Praise for *God Doesn't V*

"The story of the Fangamou family is both compelling and inspiring. Christi Pauline has done a great job of capturing the turbulent emotions of this family as they pass through trial after trial with continued trust in the Lord. It is a fascinating and rewarding read."

—John H. Groberg, General Authority Emeritus and author

"Christi Pauline has captured the tender emotions of this poignant tale of triumph over tremendous heartache. The story is moving and inspiring. The miracles that helped bring this family together remind us that we are all children of a loving Heavenly Father and that, no matter who we are, where we live, or what language we speak, He is always aware of us and will stand near to help is in our times of need. Highly recommended."

—Greg Olsen, artist

"Africa has been, and is today, a continent in turmoil. Currently there are fifteen African countries engaged in war. In our generation, millions have been butchered and killed as tribal rivalries erupted into full scale ethnic cleansing. Sadly, from Egypt to Swaziland and from Somalia to Gambia, political and tribal wars have ravaged the lives of hundreds of thousands of peace-loving families, bringing suffering and sorrow to many.

Occasionally, from this crisis of conflict and tragedy, heroes emerge. These heroes have one thing in common. They inspire us with their courage, determination, and faith in the power of love.

Christi Pauline has captured the essence of such heroism in her book, *God Doesn't Write with a Pen*, as she recounts the true story of Blema and Fatoumatou Fangamou. This story is a testimony of the triumph of the human spirit.

This story also testifies of a God of miracles. From the very first pages of this book you will find that this family, torn apart by war, was ever being guided by His hand. During a time of tremendous struggle, He softened the hearts of those who would take their lives, strengthened them physically, emotionally, and spiritually, and raised up people along the way to accomplish what they were not able to do alone by removing impossible obstacles from their path.

As the story culminates with the family coming together at last in Idaho, it brings to mind the statement of an American Prophet named Lehi: "There shall none come into this land save they shall be brought by the hand of the Lord" (2 Nephi 1:6).

This rare true story of hope, love, faith, and survival is replete with lessons of life, and can benefit all who will read it."

—John Lund, Ed.D

"Christi Pauline artfully expresses the Fangamou family's remarkable journey through both heartache and tragedy and faith and miracles. *God Doesn't Write With a Pen* is a masterful reminder that beauty, love, and hope exist in even the most unlikely of circumstances."

—Sara Wells, bestselling author

GOD DOESN'T WRITE WITH A PEN

GOD DOESN'T WRITE WITH A PEN

A True Story of Undaunted Faith and Mighty Miracles

CHRISTI LYNN PAULINE

CFI
An Imprint of Cedar Fort, Inc.
Springville, Utah

ISBN 13: 978-1-4621-1173-2

Published by CFI, an imprint of Cedar Fort, Inc.
2373 W. 700 S., Springville, UT 84663
Distributed by Cedar Fort, Inc., www.cedarfort.com

Library of Congress Cataloging in Publication data on file

Cover photo and interior map by Jonah Pauline
Cover design by Rebecca J. Greenwood & Shawnda T. Craig

Edited and typeset by Emily S. Chambers

Printed in the United States of America

10 9 8 7 6 5 4 3 2 1

Printed on acid-free paper

CONTENTS

A farmer does not conclude
by the mere look of the corn
that the corn is good;
he tears it open for examination.

—African Proverb

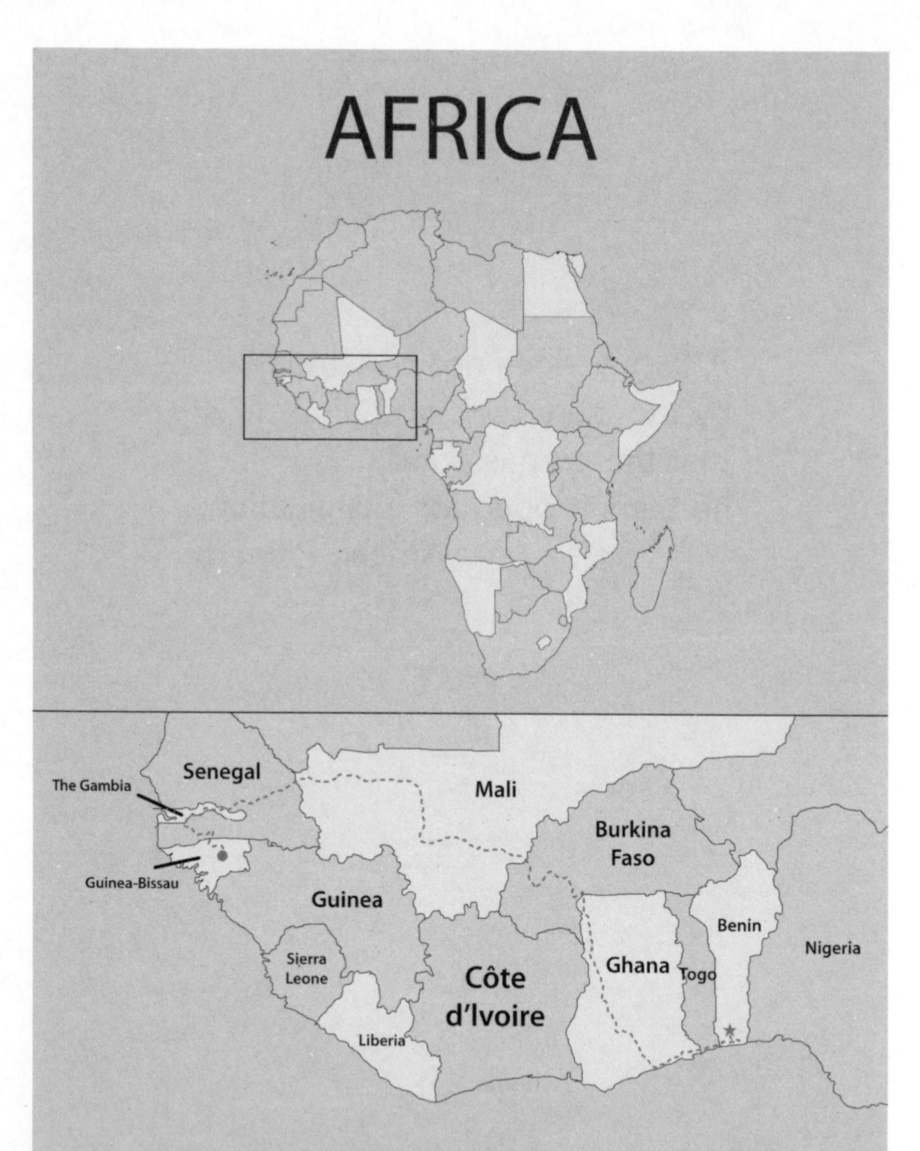

-------- Blema's route from Bafada, Guinea-Bissau to the Kpomasse Refugee Camp in Benin, a journey of aproximately 2,240 miles (3,600 kilometers). His wife, Fatoumatou, followed essentially the same route over a year later. Both walked the majority of this distance.

CHAPTER 1
The Hour of Darkness

Bafada, Guinea-Bissau, West Africa
November 23, 1998

BLEMA STOOD AT THE COUNTER OF THE PHARMACY AND TOOK OUT the heavy metal box to count the money that had come in that day. The employees had all gone home, except for Maneh, who was straightening the bottles that were lined on the shelves.

It had been a busy day. Only weeks before, a destructive bomb had exploded at a nearby hospital and had done extensive damage to the building, leaving the people with nowhere to turn for medical help. When Blema hired a few of the unemployed doctors and nurses from the Bissau hospital to work in his pharmacy in Bafada, many of the villagers had flocked there for help.

"Blema!" Maneh looked over at Blema, and, with a slight nod, motioned toward the door. Maneh had been the first to see the soldiers approach the pharmacy in their large, rusty, bullet-riddled truck as they stopped just outside the door. They held their guns close, pointed upward. There was gravity in their expressions, and he knew there was going to be trouble.

Blema looked up to see soldiers jump out of the truck and come towards the pharmacy. There was not enough time to run. "Get down!" he said, quietly but firmly. Quickly, he put the money back in the box and slipped it behind the counter as Maneh obediently lowered himself behind a shelf. Blema remained behind the counter, trying to stay calm. A shock ran through him as he saw Captain Carlos Sanha standing at the doorway.

"Carlos?" Blema looked into the eyes of his friend and was taken aback by the coldness of his icy stare. Carlos stood still, and without looking back, motioned for the other soldiers to come inside. The soldiers moved quickly as they filed into the small space. They stood, eyeing Blema like wild beasts ready to take their prey.

"Why have you been supporting the rebels, selling drugs to them?" Carlos demanded loudly.

"I sell my medications to everyone who comes into my store. There's no way for me to know who's a rebel and who's not."

"You lie!" he yelled. Without hesitation, Carlos gave the signal. One of the soldiers leapt toward Blema and struck him with the butt of his gun, leaving a deep gash on the side of his head. The force of the blow caused an intense, sharp pain that he had never felt before. As he slumped behind the counter, the room began to spin and then turned dark. When he came to, he found himself in a sea of confusion, only to be brought back to reality by the sounds of angry, blood-thirsty men as they tore through the pharmacy, pilfering the drugs and merchandise like greedy, hungry dogs.

Maneh watched, horrified, as the scene unfolded. He felt like his heart would beat right through his chest. He felt sick. Unarmed and outnumbered, he knew that there was nothing he could do to help Blema. He was sure that his employer was dead. Now he would have to try to save himself. He looked over at the open door and wondered what his chances would be of escaping. Without waiting to consider the odds, he leapt out of his hiding place and ran toward the door. The soldiers turned to see him just as he passed through the doorway. Fortunately they let him go. It was Blema that they had been sent out to kill. They turned back to Blema as he began to stir. His attacker stood just above him with his gun pointed at his head, ready to shoot.

"Stop!" Carlos commanded loudly. "Don't shoot!"

The soldier looked up with a look of defiance, angry that he had been stopped.

"What about our orders?"

"You let me worry about that," said Carlos. "You are to follow *my* orders."

The soldier reluctantly moved back just as another came toward Blema with a knife, determined to satisfy the original command.

"No!" Carlos said forcefully as he pushed the soldier away from Blema. "I said let him be! Get the drugs in the truck."

Blema lay still, taking slow, deliberate breaths while his mind raced to find a way out. He knew that he would have to move quickly and carefully if he were to escape. As the men stepped away, he moved his head toward the wall where he saw cracks of sunlight coming from an air conditioning vent. This was his only hope.

As the men were loading up the truck, Blema moved slowly and snakelike on his belly until he reached the vent and then squeezed himself into the small metal opening and worked his way through to the outer side of the wall and into the hot, sultry air outside. Holding the gash on his head, he slumped low and ran toward the bush until he was safely hidden by the thick vegetation, blood oozing down his fingers and forearms. With his mind in a fog of fear and confusion, he contemplated his next move.

His first instinct was to run home to his family, but he knew that would be a fatal mistake. Home was no longer a safe place. He had cheated death once; he might not be as fortunate a second time. The government had targeted him, and they knew where he lived. It would be only a matter of time until they caught up with him again. To stay in Guinea-Bissau meant almost certain death, and he knew he would be tempting fate to remain.

A knot formed in his gut when the thought came of leaving his family. He wanted to go to them, to protect them, but the reality was that there was no way he could stand up to a company of armed soldiers. He would be of no help to his family now. If he were to leave, however, it meant that he might not see his family again for a very long time—possibly ever. He felt weakened by the weight of the painful decision. In his heart he wanted to stay, but the voice of reason inside of him persuaded him to leave. It was with heaviness that he took the first steps toward the Senegal border, 250 kilometers away. "Lord," he cried, "please help us!"

* * * * *

Maneh didn't stop running until he arrived at Blema and Fatoumatou's house. When he arrived, Fatoumatou was standing outside, putting a pot on to boil with children running and playing at her feet. She hardly noticed the familiar sound of gunfire in the distance. She had been waiting for Blema to come home and began to wonder what was taking him so long. Bangama, her little four-year-old daughter, was eager to help her mother and gathered sticks to stoke the fire. Fatoumatou smiled at the enthusiasm of this little dark-eyed sprite. She bent down to take the sticks as a wave of nausea washed over her. She was two months into her seventh pregnancy and she had felt nauseous all day. She would be glad when this phase of the pregnancy was over.

Fatoumatou heard a faint, familiar voice calling her name from a distance and looked up to see Maneh running toward her. There was terror in his face, and she knew something was wrong.

"Children, take Bangama to the house."

"Fatoumatou," Maneh struggled to catch his breath. "Soldiers . . . they came into the pharmacy and attacked Blema . . . I saw him get hit . . . he was bleeding . . . they had guns. . . I'm afraid they've killed him . . . you and the children need to leave . . . you're not safe here!"

Fatoumatou stood and listened, trying to absorb what he was telling her. She didn't move, paralyzed by the images that were being formed in her mind as he spoke. She opened her mouth to say something, but only a high pitched squeak passed through her lips. Her hands began to tremble and Maneh took her arm and helped her to the ground.

"Maneh, what can I do? I have six children. I can't just leave my home. I wouldn't know where to go."

"I don't know, Fatoumatou. I just know that you're not safe. The soldiers are out to kill, and I don't want to see anything happen to you or the children. I'd stay and help you, but I have my own family I need to attend to."

Fatoumatou looked down and shook her head. "Yes, I understand. We'll be all right. You go home to your family."

When Maneh left, Fatoumatou went into the house and sat on a bed. She knew she needed to get a plan together, but she couldn't think straight. "Blema is dead!" she thought. Everything after that was just a haze.

The afternoon passed like a blur. Somehow, she had been able to get the children fed and had gathered them into the house. Just hours after she had received the news from Maneh, she could hear the rumble of a large vehicle roll up to her home. The children had heard it too and ran to the door. Fatoumatou stood and nervously pushed them back. With a sharper tone than she had intended, she told them to stay inside. It was dark, but as she looked out she could see the silhouettes of armed men jumping out of the truck and coming toward the house. She began to tremble as they drew near. By the time they were at the door, she could make out some of their faces. She recognized one face in particular; Carlos Sanha, a good friend of her husband. Perhaps he had come to help her. This thought calmed her down.

"FATOUMATOU!" He called. Fatoumatou cracked the door open and looked out at Carlos. There was something chillingly different about him. Although she recognized his face, this man was a stranger. Their eyes met and she was jarred by a jolt of fear that ran through her body.

Carlos pushed the door open as the soldiers followed him inside. The children huddled to one side of the room, eyes wide and following every move of the soldiers.

Without a word, the soldiers began filing into the house and going through the family's belongings, taking everything that looked of worth.

"Where's your jewelry?" Carlos demanded.

Fatoumatou just stared at him defiantly without saying a word.

"If you know what's good for you, woman, you better start talking. You can die just as easily as your husband."

Fatoumatou looked over to her children to see the terror that was in their young faces. Bangama cried as the older boys tried to comfort her.

Kamonan stepped forward. "Mother, just tell them where it is," he said in a firm voice. Fatoumatou looked at her oldest son, who was just sixteen. Until that moment she had thought of him as a child. How long, she wondered, had he possessed the strength and confidence of a man? Fatoumatou obediently yielded to his words and walked over to the small basket where her jewelry was kept.

The soldiers followed her and greedily snatched the jewelry. Then they went for everything else, loading all of the family's belongings in the truck. Within minutes the house was stripped, and she and the children stood helpless in the empty shell.

When the last thing was taken out of the house, Fatoumatou felt a strange sense of relief. The terror that took hold of her from the time the soldiers had come into the house suddenly dissipated, leaving her with a sense of gratitude. Although everything in the house was gone, she and the children were safe. No one had been hurt.

She gathered her children close to her and motioned for them to be quiet as she listened for the truck engine to start and for the intruders to drive away. Time seemed to stand still as she waited, but the only sound they could hear was that of barking dogs. Something wasn't right.

Suddenly, she heard voices. They were low and muffled at first, but the sound became louder as she listened. The soldiers hadn't left. She tensed up once again as they made their way to the house. Her eyes were fixed on the door as the men reappeared, one by one.

Fatoumatou screamed as one of the soldiers came to her and separated her from the children. He ordered the children into the bathroom and shut the door tightly behind them, leaving Fatoumatou alone with the men in the room. Her mind began to race as she searched for a way out, but there was nowhere to run; she was trapped. She began to shudder as the soldiers began circling her like a pack of hungry wolves.

"You can't give into these depraved animals" she said to herself, "You must fight."

When the soldiers left, Fatoumatou lay beaten on the floor. Her blood-soaked skirt clung to her legs where the steely sharp edges of the soldiers knives had slashed through her skin from the top of her inner thighs and down to her ankles.

As she lay there listening, the truck engine started up and began to rumble. Hot tears rolled down the side of her face as the truck backed up and slowly pulled away.

* * * * *

Terrified, Blema continued running through the bush to escape. He kept running until he could run no more. Eventually, his body gave into exhaustion, and he fell upon the ground. He didn't try to get up. He lay in the bush and slept through the night.

The next morning, he was awakened by voices of farm workers and barking dogs in the distance. For a short moment, he wondered where he was, and then he chastised himself for sleeping so long. Standing up, his muscles felt tight and ached from running. Sharp pangs of hunger gnawed at his stomach and he hoped he would find yams or root vegetables growing nearby. He stretched, brushed himself off, and then started out in the direction of the voices.

As he came near, he saw several weatherworn farm workers in a large field. The men looked up from their work when they saw him approach. There was an anxious rasp in Blema's voice as he attempted to explain his dilemma.

"I need your help." he said. "I have to get to the border."

"Why? What's going on?" one man asked.

"I've been attacked. Vieira has sent his soldiers to kill me."

"Why?"

"They think I'm supporting the rebels."

"Well, are you?"

"No! I've been working with the OSC, trying to bring peace."

The man relaxed his stance.

"I'm sorry. Any family?"

"A wife and six children. Another on the way."

"Are they okay?"

Blema's eyes fell as he slowly shook his head.

"I don't know."

The men listened to his story as if it were a familiar one.

"Things are bad, man!" another man sympathized. "But if you know where to go, I think you'll find people to help you."

Blema was given a bowl of cold rice and directions to another farm that lay a few miles to the north. The men assured him that he would not have to leave the protection of the bush to find it.

Blema thanked them and moved on. For the next four days he traveled, making his way from farm to farm, through an underground highway of sorts, which would lead him to the border.

The wound on his head had begun to heal, leaving it tender and itchy, a constant reminder of the attack. He could not keep the terrible scene from playing over and over in his mind, and he tried to make sense of it all. Anger, deep sorrow, and concern for his family weighed on him, tearing at his heart. He had to block it all out and keep his mind focused on the road ahead, determined not to stop until he was somewhere safe.

* * * * * * *

Fatoumatou lay on the floor and sobbed. Her legs and body throbbed with pain. Afraid that the men might return, she forced herself to get up off the ground. Using the already blood-soaked lapa that she was wearing, she tightly wrapped her legs to slow the bleeding. When she called out to the children, they came out timidly, their eyes wide with fright. Bangama wanted to run to her mother, but Sekouna held her back.

"Mother, are you all right?" asked Kamonan.

"I'm hurt. Help me."

"What can we do?"

"Help me up. We have to leave. We're not safe here."

"But, where will we go?" asked Mousa. The children stared at her, waiting for a response.

"I don't know. I just know that we can't stay here. I suppose we'll go where the Lord leads us. Now, help me up!"

Kamonan and Sekouna came to their mother and each supported an arm and pulled her to her feet as she grimaced with pain.

Fatoumatou thought of the money that she and Blema had been putting away for a rainy day.

"Joseph," she said. "Go outside and get the metal box your father buried by the tree and bring it to me. Thank the Lord we still have that."

When Joseph had brought her the box, she opened it and took out the five thousand francs that had been placed inside and hid the money in her clothing. With slow, careful steps, she led her children away from the house, toward the road.

They hadn't walked more than five kilometers when Fatoumatou collapsed.

A man working out in the field saw her fall from a distance and dropped his spade to run to her. The children huddled around her.

"Is this your mother?" he asked.

"Yes," Kamonan answered.

"What happened to her?"

"The soldiers came to our house. They attacked her!" Kamonan's voice began to shake with anguish and tears boiled up in his eyes as he spoke. "Will you help her?"

"Those pigs!" he spat. The man knelt down beside Fatoumatou

without speaking. He then looked back at Kamonan. "Look, son. I'd help, but I don't want any trouble. Do you understand?" Kamonan gave no response, but the man could see his disappointment. The other children were looking up at him with desperate, pleading eyes. The pitiful scene overcame him, and he relented.

"Oh, all right," he growled. "Help me lift her."

The man leaned down and lifted Fatoumatou's shoulders off the ground as the boys helped him carry her toward the hut. When the man's wife saw them coming, she ran out to help them bring her inside.

Fatoumatou was laid down on a leaf bed where the woman immediately went to work, cleaning her wounds and then wrapped her legs in a poultice. Fatoumatou was aware of what she was doing, but made no effort to speak. When the woman had finished, Fatoumatou was left alone to sleep while the children were fed and then led to a place to stay for the night.

Before the sun came up the next morning, Fatoumatou was awakened by the man who had helped her.

"Wake up!" he demanded, shaking her arm.

Fatoumatou opened her eyes. "I'm awake," she said.

"What's your name?" he asked.

"Fatoumatou."

Fatoumatou pulled herself up to a sitting position on the bed and suddenly felt anxious.

"Where are my children?" she asked.

"Don't worry, they're taken care of."

Fatoumatou breathed a sigh of relief. "Thank you. You and your wife have been very kind."

The man gave only a slight nod in response. "You're hurt pretty badly," he said, "but I'm afraid you can't stay here. You and your children will have to leave."

Fatoumatou suddenly felt vulnerable, like a small child. "But, I don't know where to go." she said timidly.

"Do you have any family outside of Guinea-Bissau?"

"Yes. I have a sister in Senegal."

"Where in Senegal?"

"She lives in Salikenhe, near Casamance. "

"Well, then I suggest you go there. . . *now*."

The man placed a strong emphasis on the word "now" and said it firmly enough to let her know that he meant it.

Fatoumatou felt a twinge of indignation. She had appreciated the man's help, but now he seemed blatantly insensitive to her condition. His compassion, it seemed, had been used up much too soon.

Fatoumatou looked directly into his eyes and could see the fear behind them. Immediately, her heart was softened. She understood his fear, and she knew it was valid. He was right; she would have to move on. Considering the distance and her painful wounds, she cringed at the thought of traveling all the way to Salikenhe, but she knew she had no choice.

"All right," she relented, "but I'll need your help."

The man leaned down as Fatoumatou put her arm around his neck. He lifted her to her feet and slowly led her outside.

The children had already been awakened and were gathered outside the door. The woman who had attended to Fatoumatou's wounds the night before stood near the doorway. As Fatoumatou stepped out of the hut, the woman looked at her apologetically. Without saying a word, she handed her a bundle of food, and with this one last gesture of kindness, Fatoumatou and her children were sent on their way.

Fatoumatou took her first steps as a stabbing pain ran through her legs. Kamonan and Sekouna ran to steady her, and she leaned on the boys as they headed back toward the road.

They had walked only a short distance when Fatoumatou saw a taxi coming down the road in the same direction. Waving her arm, she called out to the driver until he pulled up next to them. The taxi was an old, rickety wooden cart, pulled by a horse that was just as old. The driver, a stoned-faced, graying man called out, "Where you going?"

"Salikenhe," Fatoumatou replied. "Can you take us there?"

"I don't know. How much money do you have?"

"Five thousand francs."

The man shook his head. "Five thousand francs isn't going to get you to Salikenhe, Madam."

Fatoumatou knew she was in no position to haggle. "Well, then take us as far as you can."

Fatoumatou gave the man the money and climbed onto the cart. The children jumped in after her. Mousa's and Oldpa's eyes grew wide, as if they were about to embark on an adventure.

The cart began to move slowly, jostling them about as they made their way down the rutted dirt road. Traveling all day, they had gone about forty kilometers, when the driver suddenly stopped the cart and ordered them to get out.

"This is as far as I go!" he announced in a harsh tone. Fatoumatou knew there would be no point in arguing. Reluctantly, she and the children got out of the cart and began to walk.

With each step, a deep, sharp pain shot up Fatoumatou's legs, and she had to force herself to move on. The children were tired and irritable. Bangama pulled on her mother's lapa and began to cry, wanting to be held.

Fatoumatou reached down, stroking her hair. "I'm sorry, little one. I can't pick you up."

"Mama, I'm hungry!" she cried.

Bangama's whining triggered a response from the other children, and they all began to groan and complain of hunger pangs. Realizing that she too was hungry, Fatoumatou sent the boys to search for yams that grew in the fields next to the road. They wandered off, and within a half hour they came running back with several dark brown roots. They had broken them into small pieces with a rock, making sure everyone had something to eat.

By the time the sun began to set, they all were exhausted. They wandered until they had found a clearing where they could lay down and sleep.

The day had been hot and humid, and as night fell, the temperature remained warm and muggy. Their sweaty bodies seemed to attract swarms of hungry mosquitoes, and the air was filled with a loud buzz. Fatoumatou tried to use her lapa to swat them away, and then as a cover for her children, but there was no escaping the insects as they feasted on their exposed skin. The attacks continued throughout the night, and by morning they had gotten little sleep. They were tired, swollen, and itchy.

When the sun came up, the family reluctantly arose to resume their travel. By mid-morning, the sun was already beating down on them, and they became unbearably thirsty and dehydrated from exposure to the sun's rays. They searched for clean water, but it was not to be found. With no other choice, they were forced to drink from the filthy pools they found along the way, and it made them feel nauseated.

Food was hard to find, and in the days ahead, they ate only what they could glean from the fields or beg from a sympathetic stranger they would pass on the road. It was never enough and they were constantly hungry.

With nowhere to bathe, after nearly three weeks of walking, the dirt had ground into their skin and their hair was matted and stiff. Their sweaty bodies had developed a stench. They were sore and tired, and their legs were swollen well beyond their normal size. When at last they reached the border, they were relieved to think that they were coming close to the journey's end. It had not yet occurred to Fatoumatou that they might not make it across the border.

* * * * *

After four days of walking, Blema stood on the Guinea-Bissau side of the Senegal border. He knew it was not the time to let his guard down; this would be the most critical part of the journey, and there was no room for errors.

Following directions he had been given, he worked his way to a remote section where he could avoid an encounter with the border guards. Once he was at the border, he looked in every direction until he was assured that he was alone.

"Oh, Lord," he pleaded. "Help me!"

With his heart beating wildly, he ran with all of his might until he had made his way across. He didn't stop running until he could run no longer. At last, he fell to his knees, relieved that he had made it.

Blema was filled with a sense of euphoria, having come to a place where he could feel safe. After a short rest, he picked himself up off of the ground and continued walking.

When he had gone several miles, he came upon a dirt road and followed it until it led him to a small village. As he came near the huts, several of the villagers saw him and stopped what they were doing. They stared at him as he passed by, making him suddenly conscious of his appearance. He was sweaty and unbathed, and his clothes were dirty and torn in places. He knew that he must be a quite a sight.

A man carrying a pail of water passed by and looked at him suspiciously and then stopped. Reaching for his cup, he dipped it into the water and held it out to him.

"Here," he said, "You look like you could use this."

"Yes. Thank you."

Blema took the cup and began gulping the water. The cool liquid offered pleasant relief as it made its way down his dry throat. The man watched curiously as he drank.

"Quite a stir in Guinea-Bissau," he stated, as if to make casual conversation.

"Oh, yeah?" Blema replied, wiping the moisture from his lips. "What's going on?"

"Do you know General Ansumane Mane, army chief of staff?

"I've heard of him. Why?"

"Well, I hear that President 'Nino' Vieira has fired him. Accused him of illegally selling arms and land mines to Senegalese rebels. Now it seems that Vieira has convinced Senegal leaders to watch for Guinea-Bissau rebels making their way across the border, to have them sent back or have them killed."

The man leaned closer to Blema, lowering his voice. "There's a refugee camp called Kpomasse in Benin. It's run by the United Nations, and they're taking in refugees from all over West Africa. You might consider going there."

Blema stepped back. "I am not a rebel!"

The man shrugged his shoulders. "Didn't say you were."

Blema handed back the man's cup and turned and walked away.

Although Blema had never been involved in the rebel movement, he knew that Vieira considered him to be a rebel sympathizer. He had ordered his soldiers to kill him in Guinea-Bissau. Now it seemed that even here in Senegal, he was not safe. The sense of euphoria that he had felt had been short lived.

As Blema continued on, he thought about what the man had said, and he knew that he was right; he would have to move on. The Kpomasse camp seemed a reasonable place to go, but Benin was so far away, almost two thousand kilometers. He would need a plan.

Mapping out a route, Blema decided that the best way for him to get to Benin would be to travel from Senegal to Mali and then on to Burkina Faso. From there he would continue through Ghana and Togo and then to Benin where he would look for the Kpomasse camp. Although this seemed to be the shortest route, it was still very far away. Walking that distance would be extremely difficult.

A train was available from Senegal to Mali. Blema knew that if he took the train, he could get out of the country quickly, but that would require money, and he had none. The only valuable thing he had left in his possession was a watch that had been given to him by his brother, Kamonan. He looked at his watch and wondered how much he could sell it for. He might be able to get enough money to buy some food and a ticket to Mali.

As he mulled over the idea of selling his watch, a sense of sadness came over him. It would be difficult to part with it. It was the only really nice thing that he had ever owned, and now it was the only material thing he had left to remind him of the life that he had just left behind. But the reality was, he needed food, and he had to get out of Senegal. He knew what he had to do.

Blema proceeded cautiously through the village, asking if someone might be interested in buying his watch. Everyone he approached seemed to be interested, but no one had money. Someone had made mention of a man who bought and sold merchandise for a living, and Blema decided to go and look for him.

The man wasn't hard to find. He stood on a street corner, loudly peddling his wares. Blema walked up to him and held out his watch. The man took it from him and studied it carefully, turning it over and over in his hands.

"How much do you want for it?" the man asked.

"How much are you willing to pay?"

The man's face remained expressionless as he looked the watch over once again. "It's not worth much," he murmured. "I'll give you ten thousand francs for it." Blema looked at him in disbelief. Without a word, he reached over, took his watch back, and turned to leave. He had gone only a few steps before the man called out, "fifteen thousand francs!" Blema turned around. "I won't take less than thirty thousand." The two men began to bicker back and forth until they finally settled on twenty-five thousand francs.

In the end, Blema knew that he had sold the watch for less than it was worth, but with the money he would be able to obtain food, supplies, and a one-way ticket to Mali, the first leg of the journey. His stay in Senegal had lasted only two days before he moved on.

* * * * *

With the border check station in sight, Fatoumatou stood with her children, watching the guards pace back and forth around the small cinderblock building that had been set up. They were in uniform, their gun straps draped over their shoulders, smoking cigarettes and talking casually to one another. Fatoumatou was seized by fear at the sight of them. Until now, she hadn't really thought of the possibility of not being able to cross the border, and the thought made her feel a sense of panic. If she and the children were not allowed to pass through, she wondered how they would survive. The journey had taxed all of their bodies to their limits, and she didn't know how much further they could go on.

Fatoumatou stood still and prayed silently until a sense of calm came over her. Then, with quickened resolve, she stood up and courageously proceeded to walk straight toward the guards with her children close behind.

"Where are you going?" Fatoumatou was startled by the loud, sharp voice of the guard. Suddenly, all of her courage melted away. She tried to speak, but couldn't.

"Answer me!" he barked.

"We're going to my sister's house." Fatoumatou's voice was trembling. "She lives in Salikenhe."

"What's your sister's name?"

"Kadiatou Diallo. She lives there with her husband and children."

"Where are you coming from?"

"Bafada."

"Bafada? You've come a long way, woman! Where's your husband?"

Fatoumatou hesitated, finding it difficult to form the words. "He's been killed. We've been forced from our home and don't have anywhere else to go."

Fatoumatou was suddenly overcome by emotion and exhaustion, and she dropped to her knees. Without the strength to pick herself back up, she bent her head to the ground.

The guard looked at her pitifully and then down at the children. Suddenly, the hardness of his countenance softened.

"All right," he said with a more gentle tone. "Bring your children. We'll see what we can do."

Fatoumatou was taken aback by his unexpected response and lifted her head. For a moment she wasn't sure if she had heard him right.

"Sir?"

"You heard me. Bring your children. I'll make sure you get to your sister's house."

Without hesitation, Sekouna went to his mother and helped her get up off the ground.

The guard walked briskly back to the building where he telephoned the immigration officials. When he asked for their assistance, they agreed to send transportation.

As promised, a van soon arrived. Fatoumatou and the children got in and they were taken to where Kadiatou lived.

Kadiatou was outside cooking when the van pulled up next to the house. As the door opened and Fatoumatou and the children stepped out, Kadiatou could only stare, shocked by her sister's appearance and the condition of the children.

"Fatoumatou!" she finally exclaimed. "What's happened to you?"

Fatoumatou was unable to answer. Kadiatou dropped what she was doing and came running to her, pulling her into a tight embrace. The children watched as the sisters held one another and wept.

Kadiatou then flew into a flurry of action, gathering food and clothing for Fatoumatou and the children, seeing to it that they were fed, bathed, and had clean, dry clothes to wear.

Kadiatou and her husband, Therno, were concerned about Fatoumatou. She was now in her third month of pregnancy, and it was apparent to them that she was not doing well. Her wounds had become infected and were oozing, and she was suffering from a headache, nausea, and diarrhea—all symptoms of malaria. They were deeply concerned for the baby as well. They tried to convince her that she needed to go to the hospital where she could be cared for, but knowing that there was no way for her to pay for such extravagant care, she refused to go.

Over the next few days, Fatoumatou's condition worsened until she realized she had no choice. Therno helped her into town where she was admitted into the hospital in Casamance.

Kadiatou and Therno's suspicions had been right, Fatoumatou had contracted malaria. She would spend the next three months in the hospital recovering, while her children remained in Kadiatou's care. Fatoumatou felt greatly indebted to Kadiatou and Therno. She didn't know what she would have done without them.

* * * * *

The money that Blema received from selling his watch didn't go far. As soon as he got off the train in Mali, he began to look for work.

It was January, the beginning of the dry season. The time of harvest was past, and the ground now lay dormant. Since it was still too early to plant, Blema knew that work would be hard to come by. Nevertheless, as he made his way from farm to farm to ask for work, he was disappointed when no one would hire him. After several days of searching, he became discouraged and decided it would be best to move on.

Traveling had become slow, as now it was done mostly on foot. By the time he finally crossed over the Mali border into Burkina Faso, he was desperate to find work. He was greatly relieved when he saw that the farmers were beginning to prepare the ground for planting, and it wasn't long before he was able to find work at a cassava farm.

When he was hired on, it was with the understanding that he would be there for only a short time, or the time it took him to save the money he needed for another bus ticket to the next city. His employer had agreed, and he went to work immediately.

Blema joined the other farm hands the next morning at the crack of dawn. He was glad that they had started work early, while the air was still cool. By ten o'clock, the sun was already glaring down on the workers. By mid-afternoon, it had become torturous. Doing his best to ignore his discomfort, Blema continued to work alongside the others until nightfall, and by then, he was at the point of exhaustion.

At the end of the day, he left the fields and found someone he could barter with for something to eat. He had little to barter with, so he had little to eat. He then made his way to the commercial parking lot where he would bed down on a piece of cardboard for the night.

The dirt parking lot had become a popular camping spot at night for those who were on the road. Blema joined a group of strangers and claimed his spot on the hard ground. Because some of the men were of questionable character, he found a heavy stick and laid it beside him for protection. He knew that it would be impossible to sleep well, but even so, when the morning came, he would get up early, brush himself off, and set out to do it all over again.

Blema continued to work at the farm for three weeks, and then, with a small amount of money in his pocket and his rolled up piece of cardboard, he hit the road once again. He traveled as far as he could until the money ran out, and then began looking for work again. Working a few days here and a few weeks there, he steadily made his way toward Benin.

After traveling hundreds of miles, he finally reached Togo, and having found work at a millet farm, he decided to stay until the end of the season.

While in Togo, Blema had come to feel that he was relatively safe, but he also felt desperately alone. Not a day had gone by when his heart did not ache for Fatoumatou and the children. He thought of them constantly and missed them terribly. He prayed unceasingly for their well-being. He also thought of his mother and knew that she would be beside herself with worry.

While thinking of his mother one day, his mind began to drift back to the days of his boyhood, and for the first time in a long time, he began to smile.

CHAPTER 2
Beginnings

Bambadinga, Guinea-Bissau, West Africa
January 1959

LIFE IN THE BEGINNING WAS SIMPLE. IT HAD STARTED OUT IN THE small village of Bambadinga, where Blema's boyhood home was surrounded by old trees and clumps of thirsty vegetation. It was here, in a little round mud hut with a dry thatch roof that his life had begun. Blema had been told the story of his birth many times before, and he knew it well.

The event had taken place on a moonlit night in January. It was during the dry season when the West African rains had ceased and the torrid air had sucked the life out of every green thing, leaving the land parched and dry. After the dust and the blistering heat of the day had settled, the night became calm and pleasant, filled with sounds of loud chirping insects. And then, in the midst of the calm, there was a cry.

As the blue night slowly gave way to the dawn, the rhythmic sounds of drums seemed to rise up from nowhere and could be heard throughout the village, signifying the event. It was on this night that his mother held her baby for the very first time.

Seven days later, he was given the name of Blema. He was named after his father, Blemou, which meant "gatherer or nurturer."

Blema always felt that this name fit his father. This gentle patriarch was the magnet that pulled his family and friends together. He seemed to watch over them as a shepherd watches over his precious sheep, seeing to it that they were fed and happy. Blema liked this about his father and hoped this trait had been passed down with the name.

Blema's father was a plain man, a rural subsistence farmer who made his living off the land, growing rice, groundnuts, corn, bananas, pineapples, potatoes, and yams, and he raised chickens and goats. He and his family made their home in two round mud houses, with the males living in one house and the women in the other. The floors were dirt. The beds were made of dried leaves.

According to Blemou, it had been a windfall of good fortune that his son had been born into the Mandinka tribe. Theirs was a strong tribe, among the largest in Guinea-Bissau, and it was one of which they could be proud to be a part.

Blema would learn, however, that the strength of his people had not come without a price. History tells of a tribe that had survived a troubled past, marked by centuries of tribulation and oppression. After the Portuguese won control over Guinea-Bissau in the 1500s, nearly two million people were sold into slavery over the next two centuries. One third of those were Mandinka, which had a tremendous impact on the tribe.[1]

Yet, in spite of their troubles, the tribe proudly maintained their history, customs, and rich traditions, distinct from the Fula, Pepel, Makangni, Bizoko, Balanta, Zebe, Djakanke, and Madjako tribes that surround them.

From as far back as he could remember, Blema was taught by his father what it meant to be Mandinka. When he was barely six years old, Blemou came to him one day and solemnly announced, "Blema, it's time for you to become a man!"

Small for his age, Blema's little body trembled with fear and excitement as his father explained the importance of circumcision. His little-boy mind couldn't fully comprehend the reasons for the event, but he felt that he would be participating in something very important, and it made him feel grown up and proud.

This, he was told, would be one of the most significant events of his life. All the boys and girls within the tribe would have their genitalia cut between the ages of four and fourteen, marking the beginning of adulthood.

In his father's day, the children would spend up to a year in the bush after being circumcised, but that had changed. His father had assured him that he would only stay for the time it took for him to heal, about three weeks. While in the bush, he would be cared for and taught by the elders. The older children would learn adult social responsibilities and rules of behavior within the tribe, while the other younger children would learn stories and songs about how to behave in their families and of the ways of the Mandinka.[2]

Blema would come to feel a special bond of love with the elders who taught him in the bush. Despite the horror of being cut, he would always look back at the event with fondness.

Blema's mother, Vassi Saourohara, was a busy woman. With five young children running underfoot, she somehow managed to do the cooking and cleaning, washing the clothes, hauling water, and taking care of the garden. It was also her responsibility to make the trek to the village market with the other women to trade the crops for other food and other necessities.

Blema had a soft spot in his heart for his mother. Vassi was a kind and caring woman with a big heart and pleasant demeanor. Known as a peacemaker at home and throughout the village, she always seemed to go out of her way to get along with everyone around her, avoiding conflict like the plague.

It was hard for Blema and his siblings not to try to take advantage of her good nature sometimes, but whenever they tried, they found that there was just enough toughness in her to keep them in line.

Blema was especially fond of his mother's cooking. She had a magical way of transforming the most simple and common ingredients into mouthwatering dishes, which almost always included rice or fufu and some kind of vegetable, such as tomatoes, peppers, onions, casaba, yams, or carrots, or whatever else she could get her hands on. When times were good or on special occasions, the family was treated with meat, such as chicken, goat, lamb, or fish. Beef was rarely seen, reserved for those with money.

Blema was a bright child, and his young heart burned with a desire to learn. Although education had been denied most citizens during Portuguese rule, it was later made available after Guinea-Bissau had gained its independence in 1973, but it was not free. Most families could not afford to send their children to school.

Not only was Blema's father unable to afford sending his children to school, he didn't believe it was necessary, or at least not worth the great sacrifices that would be required to send them.

"Haven't I always put food in your mouth?" Blemou insisted whenever the subject came up. "I never went to school and my family has always been fed."

Blema's brothers and sisters seemed to accept the fact that they wouldn't be going to school, and he wished at times that he could be as accepting. But as much as he tried, he just couldn't seem to let go of his dream.

As the years rolled by, Blema held on to this hope, but he was disappointed again and again when the opportunity didn't come. By the time he turned twelve, he felt that it had grown too late.

About that time, there was an uncle on his mother's side named Sori, who had become ill and had sent to have one of Blemou and Vassi's children come to his home in Guinea-Conakry to help. He had singled out Blema, but Blema's mother was hesitant to let him go.

"We can't let him go, Blemou!" Blema's mother had told his father. Her voice had become loud and shrill, the way it always did when she was upset.

"Vassi, listen." Blemou tried to calm and reason with her. "Your brother is very sick and needs help. You know how he favors Blema. Blema is mature for his age and could do a good job."

"Yes, I know he would, but he's never been away from us for that long. He's still a boy. What if the work is too hard for him?"

"Blema is twelve years old. He needs to learn to work. Besides that, you know that times are hard for us right now. Having him go live with your brother for a while would mean one less mouth to feed."

Vassi couldn't argue with that. Blema was glad when she agreed to let him go. Although he was apprehensive about leaving his home and family, he was proud of the fact that, out of all of his siblings and cousins, he was the one who had been chosen to care for his uncle. With nothing but a change of clothing and the good advice from his parents, he was sent on his way.

When Blema arrived at Sori's home, he was put to work right away. He took his responsibilities seriously and worked hard, doing whatever was asked of him.

Sori towered over the young boy's small frame, and it took a great effort to care for him. Determined to accomplish what he had been sent there to do, Blema moved his uncle, cleaned him, dressed him, and accompanied him to the bathroom. Occasionally the family would feel sorry for him and stepped in to help, but mostly he bore the responsibility on his own.

When he was not caring for Sori, Blema was put to work around the house and property. He helped with the gardening, hauled the wood, and carried water. In time, what had started out for him as an adventure ended up feeling more like drudgery. Although he loved this family dearly, he felt that he had become their servant boy, and it wasn't long before discouragement set in.

To add to his discontent, his cousin Mama, who was also twelve, was attending school. While Blema was doing the difficult work around the house, Mama was off learning new and exciting things. She would come running home from school each day and look for him until she had found him, then excitedly exclaim, "Blema, guess what I learned in school today!" She might as well have had stabbed him in the heart. Day after day he was tortured by her teasing and was painfully tormented by the injustice of it all.

One day, while feeling particularly sorry for himself, Blema went to his uncle and asked if he would consider giving him the same privilege as his cousin. He wanted to go to school with her.

"I'm sorry, Blema," Sori answered firmly, "That is not for you!"

Blema went off by himself and cried.

Over the next few days, the problem consumed him. He stopped eating and drinking, and he refused to do his chores. After several days, Sori came to him and demanded to know the reason for his changed behavior. Through his tears, Blema poured out his heart and explained why it was important for him to go to school. He reminded his uncle of how hard he had worked and pointed out that he had done all that had been required of him. Now that his uncle had seen some improvement in his health and did not require all of his time, Blema felt that it was only right that his request was at least considered.

Blema's words struck a chord with his uncle and seemed to crack the hard shell around his heart. He was surprised when Sori began to cry along with him.

"Blema, you're right," he told him. "You deserve an education!"

Blema was soon admitted into the Ecole Priemiere Mamadou Konate in Guinea-Conakry.

Over the next few years, Blema continued to live with Sori and his family during the school year and then returned home to be with his family during the school break. He remained at home for three months until school started again in September. He always looked forward to spending that time with his family; he missed them greatly.

* * * * *

School break fell at the beginning of the rainy season when Blema's father was preparing to plant. Blemou knew that if the gods were good to him, the ground that had lain barren since December would soon be soaked by monsoonal-type downpours, and the earth would thirstily drink up enough water to sustain the land through the growing season and into the dry season. Because Blemou's livelihood depended upon what he could grow, he was not about to leave his success to chance. Every year, he made offerings to the gods to ensure a prosperous growing season.

Like Blemou's father and grandfather before him, Blemou practiced Voodoo. He believed that the spirits of his dead ancestors lived side by side with those in the world of the living, and that they were ever present in the affairs of their daily lives. He connected with them through rituals using fetishes, including statues and dried animal parts.

According to Blemou's belief, each family line possessed its own priesthood. This priesthood had been passed down to them from their ancestors, from father to son for generations. When Blemou received this priesthood from his father, he also became the recipient of a mask that had been made by his grandfather.

The mask was made of wood and carved with intricate detail, and it had become the center of their rituals. It was believed that the mask held certain spiritual powers and that through it, they would be able to connect with their ancestors to call down blessings of protection, guidance, healing, and prosperity.

Every year, at the beginning of planting season, Blemou would gather his wife and children together around a small wooden table outside the hut. On the table he would place the mask, a cola nut, and a dead chicken. The children watched with fascination as their father proceeded with the ritual and called upon their ancestors. Blema and his siblings participated by joining in the prayers and singing songs they had been taught.

There were hundreds of thousands of people who practiced Voodoo in West Africa, and yet, it was only one of the many mystic religions in that region. The majority of the people were Muslim. Because there were very few Christians, Blema was not exposed to Christianity until he began attending school.

* * * * *

Blema became acquainted with two Christian boys that were in his class at school. One boy belonged to the Evangelical Church, while the other was Pentecostal. Both had invited him to attend their churches. While Blema had no intention of becoming involved in either church, he accepted the invitations out of politeness.

When Blema attended the Evangelical church, he became intrigued by what was being taught there. The unfamiliar doctrine seemed to spark an interest in him, and he soon felt a strong desire to know more about Christianity. The minister gave him a Bible, and from the moment he began reading it, he didn't want to put it down. The words of the book sank deep within his heart, and in time, he became convinced that what he read was true. This newfound knowledge excited him, and he couldn't wait to share it with his father.

"Because of school, they have spoiled your brain!" Blemou had bellowed when he told him about the things he had learned. "I knew it was a mistake to allow you to attend that school!"

"Father, please just listen," he had pleaded, "this is important!"

"You've said enough, Blema! Those people are filling your brain with nonsense. I don't need to hear any more."

Because of his father's sensitivity on the matter, it would be several years before Blema would declare himself to be a Christian.

* * * * * * *

Blema continued to attend school, eventually earning a GED certificate from the College d'Enseignment Ruale de Debreka in Guinea-Conakry.

In his final year of high school, all of the students in his class were required to take a national examination. This aptitude test would determine the type of training that would best match his skills and abilities if he chose to continue with schooling.

When the results from his test came back, he was told that he should go into agriculture.

"Agriculture!" Blema groaned. "But, I've worked hard to get an education so I could get away from farming. Isn't there anything else I can do?"

"I don't know what that would be, Blema," the school principal had said. "Your test scores indicate that you would be best suited for agriculture."

"There has to be something else," Blema insisted.

The principle thought for a moment. "Well, come to think of it, perhaps there is. I've just learned of an air traffic control training course that's being offered by a French instructor here in Guinea-Conakry. Your math scores are high enough; perhaps with a little persuasion, I could get them to take you. Would you be interested in doing something like that?"

Blema straightened up in his chair. Just the sound of the title, *air traffic controller*, made his heart skip a beat.

"Yes, Sir! I would like that very much!"

Blema was soon accepted into the program and became part of a group of young eager students at the academy.

For the next two years, he ate, drank, and breathed air traffic control. Inspired by his instructor, he strived to learn everything he could about the profession, and in 1979, he completed the course.

Blema's first job as an air traffic controller was at the Guinea-Conakry airport. He liked the job, but he missed his family, and it began to tug at his heart. Wanting to be closer to home, he applied for a position with the Guinea-Bissau Airport. After several weeks, to his delight, he was hired.

"Blema, are you in love?" his brother had teased one day.

"What? Why are you asking me that?"

"Because of the way you've been flittering around here, singing."

"Well, okay, if you must know, I *am* in love . . . with my job!"

The job was challenging and exhilarating. The people he worked with were interesting, and the environment was clean and enjoyable. He even loved the smell of the airport. The pay was not so good, but that didn't matter. The work gave him a sense that he was doing something important with his life. He had found his niche and was content.

Blema's father was impressed with his son's accomplishments.

"I'm very proud of you, Blema!" he had said one day, with a hardy slap on his shoulder.

"Thank you, Father. That means a lot to me." It was wonderful to feel the approval of his father.

"We will celebrate your new job!" Blemou exclaimed. "Tomorrow we will gather the family together and I will call upon our ancestors for a blessing. This will assure you success in your new career."

Blema hesitated, not knowing how to respond. He and his father had not spoken of religion since the day his father had learned he was a Christian. Blema choose his words carefully, afraid that what he was about to say would offend his father.

"I know you mean well, Father, but I can't participate in a Voodoo blessing."

His father bristled.

"What are you talking about? Are you now too good for a father's blessing?"

"No! Of course not. I just don't believe in praying to a mask."

"Is that right? Well, what exactly do you believe, Blema? You have become arrogant and disrespectful, and now you have dishonored our ancestors."

"I don't mean to dishonor anyone, Father. I have great respect for you and our ancestors, but I can't worship them. I believe that the God of Abraham is the one who hears our prayers. He is the true God. If you want to continue to worship the mask, I know I can't do anything to stop you, but I can't participate in it."

"I see . . . now you are too good for a blessing! What else are you too good for, Blema?" Not waiting for an answer, Blemou spun and walked away.

Blema watched his father leave and he felt like a little boy. He knew he had hurt him. He wanted to run after him and tell him that everything was all right and that he had changed his mind, but he knew he couldn't. Deep down, he knew what he had done was right and that he would have to stand his ground, as hard as that would be. As much as Blema didn't want to disappoint his father, he didn't want to offend God by worshiping the mask.

Blema's older brother, Kounan, was standing nearby and had overheard the conversation. He ran to catch up with his father.

"Father, I don't understand what's going on with Blema," he said, "but I would feel honored if you would give me your blessing."

Blemou's face softened as he looked at his oldest son. Kounan understood. He put his arm around his neck and embraced him.

"Yes, son, of course!"

The next day, all were gathered around the table, except for Blema. The mask was set in its place in the center of the table, along with the kola nuts and chicken. With everything set, Blemou cried out to his ancestors, asking them to pour down a blessing upon his son, to endow him with health, wealth, and prosperity.

Kounan appreciated the blessing of his father. He had been in pursuit of his own career dreams, working toward owning a pharmacy in Guinea-Bissau. He had taken a job at the Ivory Coast, which had enabled him to support his family and put some money away toward his goal. His wife had been supportive of his idea, even though it meant having him gone for weeks at a time, leaving her to care for the children. Now that Kounan had received a blessing, they believed the ancestors would help him fulfill his dream.

When Kounan returned to his job, he knew immediately that something was wrong. His employer was waiting for him when he came in to work, and he took him aside to speak with him. Kounan knew by the look on his face that it was not going to be good news.

"I'm sorry, Kounan," his employer said regretfully. "But we won't be needing you anymore."

Kounan stood and looked at him in disbelief. "What do you mean? Haven't I been doing a good job?"

"Yes, you're a good worker, but times are hard. I'm afraid that we just don't have the work right now."

"But, I really need this job. My family is depending on it."

"There's nothing I can do, Kounan. I'm sorry."

It was a long road back to Guinea-Bissau. Kounan's heart was in turmoil as he tried to reconcile his misfortune with the blessing he had been given by his father. Upon his return, Kounan searched for his father until he found him in the orchard.

"Father, I've been sacked!" he announced.

Blemou looked up at his son. Kounan's face revealed his hurt and confusion.

"I'm sorry, son," said Blemou.

"I don't understand it, Father. How could I have lost my job after I received the blessing?"

Kounan's question was met with an empty stare. Blemou shared his son's confusion and didn't know how to comfort him.

"I don't know, Kounan."

"Perhaps Blema was right." Kounan asserted. "Maybe the mask is just a mask, and his God is the true God."

The comment struck Blemou in an already sensitive spot. As he listened to his son, the hurt and anger swelled up inside him once again.

"You don't know what you're saying, Kounan!" he said loudly. "Your brother has abandoned his beliefs to follow after some crazy foreign idea. Now are you going to share his doubts?"

Kounan gazed at the ground as his father spoke. "I just don't know what to believe anymore, Father."

With no more to be said, the two parted in silence.

Kounan went to Blema and told him what had happened and related the conversation that he had with their father. Blema felt bad that Kounan had lost his job and was sorry that his father had lashed out at him. He also felt hurt by the things his father had said about him.

"I don't understand everything, Kounan," he said, "I just know what I believe." Blema picked up his Bible and handed it to his brother. "You might find what you're looking for in this."

Kounan took the book home with him and began to read it. In time, he too became a Christian.

* * * * *

Kounan eventually found other employment closer to home and saved his money until he was able to purchase a building and start a pharmacy. The older building had been cleaned and painted, shelves had been built and stocked with medications and merchandise, and the doors were opened for business. The only thing he lacked was a good employee.

"Blema, I have a proposition for you," Kounan announced one day. "How would you like to come and work for me in the pharmacy?"

"Thanks for the offer, but I already have a good job."

"I know that, Blema, but listen. You could do much better in the pharmacy."

"No, Kounan. I'm afraid you'll have to find someone else. I like my job. I'll stay where I am."

"It's not a matter of liking it, Blema. You might have prestige as an air traffic controller, but your pockets will always be empty. How will you ever support a wife and a family? You'd be better off coming to work for me."

"Look, I know you're trying to look out for me, and I appreciate that, but I've worked hard to get the position at the airport. This is what I want to do with my life. I'm happy where I am!"

Blema's mother busied herself around the hut while listening to her boys discuss the matter.

"Blema," she said, "you need to listen to your brother. What he's saying makes sense. He knows what's best for you."

"Blema," Kounan continued, "the pharmacy is an interesting field, and you'll have opportunities to move up. Eventually you could go to school and become a pharmacy tech., and besides that, I need you there. I know you would be a good employee."

Blema was silent. He knew that he had been defeated. He stood no chance of winning any discussion when his mother and brother joined forces, and deep down, he knew his brother was right.

Before long, he was employed at the pharmacy. Although it took some time to adjust to his new career, he was glad that he had listened to his brother. Kounan was equally appreciative that Blema had sacrificed his dream to help him out. To show his gratitude, one day he presented him with a watch.

"Blema, I want you to take this," he said as he held out the watch.

Blema took it and turned it over in his hands. He had never seen a watch as beautiful. The bold face was set in a deep gold casing, with a gold band to match. He ran his finger along the edge of the gold casing and was speechless.

"I know how much you've given up to work here, Blema," Kounan said with heartfelt sincerity. "I want you to know how much that means to me."

Blema was touched by Kounan's kind gesture, and he knew that he would always treasure the watch.

Blema felt good about his situation at the pharmacy. To his surprise, the work had become fascinating and gratifying, and he felt optimistic about his future. Now, with a secure job and a way to support a wife and family, he could think of only one thing . . . Fatoumatou!

CHAPTER 3
A Chosen Wife

Fatoumatou Diallo was five years old when her father promised her to Blema Fangamou, son of Blemou. It would take years for her to really understand what that meant for her. Her destiny, it seemed, had been irrevocably decided for her from the beginning.

She knew she shouldn't complain; this was just the way it was in Bafada amongst her people. Still, she couldn't help but wonder what it would be like to be able to choose a husband for herself. It wasn't that she had anything against Blema. He seemed nice enough. Certainly her father had put a lot of thought into the decision, and he had chosen to do what he felt would be in her best interest, out of love for her. Fatoumatou adored her father and wanted to trust that he had done well by her. Her father and Blemou had known each other for a very long time, and they had developed a strong bond of friendship. The arrangement of marriage between their children would further strengthen that bond, making them family.

The marriage between her and Blema would not become official until she became of age, of course—at least fourteen—and then only if she agreed to it. She knew that she would not be forced to accept the arrangement, but she also knew it would be extremely difficult to back out. Her father's honor was at stake. He would be put to shame if she chose not to go through with the marriage, and she could not do that to him. It would be easier to endure an unwanted marriage through a lifetime than to bring shame to her father. She would try to accept the arrangement, and she told herself that everything would be all right.

Her father, Mamadou Aliou Diallo, was a wealthy man, at least by Fula standards. He made his living as a pastoralist, keeping cattle, sheep, goats, and chickens.

Mamadou was a good man, a man of principle, and highly respected in his community. He was Muslim and he had taken two wives—Fatoumatou's mother and another woman. According to the traditions of that region, he was allowed to have up to four wives as long as he could care for them equally. Mamadou prided himself on providing well for his wives and children. He governed the family and business affairs well, and he directed all of their religious observances.

The women often worked together throughout the day, but they occupied separate huts, along with their children. These large, round huts were made of block, overlaid with a stucco-like covering and washed over with white paint. The roofs were dry thatch.

Fatoumatou's mother, Mariama, was strong and handsome. She had given Mamadou seven children: five boys and two girls. Eight more children were born to Mamadou's second wife, making him the father of fifteen children in all.

Fatoumatou was Mariama's third child, and she resembled her mother more than her siblings. She was tall and lean with sharp, pronounced features and strong bones. Her face had a radiant glow, showing off her high cheekbones and flawless forehead. Unlike her mother however, Fatoumatou had a naturally sweet, easy temperament.

Life had been hard on Fatoumatou's mother. Early marriage, followed by years of toiling in the African sun, working in the garden, fetching water, cooking, cleaning, washing and mending clothes, hauling wood, and bearing and caring for children had taken a toll on her, and it all seemed to rob her of the joy she had possessed in her youth. The years had left her feeling tired and frustrated. Unfortunately, her frustration was often taken out on her children.

Mariama was a strict disciplinarian and she had no patience for idleness. All of her children knew to stay busy if they were to remain in her good graces.

As young girls, Fatoumatou and her sister, Kadiatou, were taught to do many of the chores around the house and in the garden. Like their mother, they learned to work hard. Not all the chores were a burden, however. Fatoumatou and Kadiatou loved to help their mother cook, especially when making fufu.

When making this common dish, the girls would peel the cassava or yams and then throw them into a big pot of boiling water that was placed just above the fire. When the vegetables were tender, they would take turns pounding and mashing the soft pulp with mortars and pestles. Moving up and down, they kept a steady rhythm with their long pestles as if they were doing a dance. They continued pounding until the pulp had a playdough-like consistency.

When the family gathered to eat, everyone would pinch off a small bit of fufu and form it into a ball and then press the center with their thumbs. The indention was filled with soup their mother had made, usually with okra, fish, or tomato.

Fatoumatou loved this time of day when her family came together to enjoy the food and share stories. The evening conversation often centered on the events of the day, but sometimes her brothers would tell tales of strange people and places, giving her a sense that there was much more beyond the life she knew in Guinea-Bissau.

The greatest storyteller in her family was her father. He had a way of making his stories come alive. She liked listening to his parables as he taught his children how to behave honorably and live peacefully with one another. He often took this time to read from the Quran, impressing upon their young minds the importance of following its teachings.

Fatoumatou was mesmerized by her father's low, droning voice as he read. It lulled and comforted her. His voice was one of reason and wisdom, and she felt safe when she heard it.

Mamadou wanted for each of his children to learn to read and write Arabic so they could read the Quran on their own. Arrangements had been made with an instructor to teach them. When Fatoumatou turned seven, she was permitted to join her older siblings at their instructor's home.

Each morning before the sun came up, she and the other children would rise, do their morning chores, and then walk several miles to his home. Once they had arrived, they were tutored for several hours and then returned home in the afternoon to resume their chores until dinnertime.

Fatoumatou's brothers were allowed to continue with their schooling into their late teens. Fatoumatou and her sisters, on the other hand, were only permitted to take part in the class until they reached the age of menstruation—thirteen or fourteen. Then they were expected to stay home and prepare themselves for marriage.

"You will make a good wife someday, Fatoumatou," her father would often tell her.

"How will you ever expect to be a good wife, Fatoumatou?" were the words that she heard from her mother.

As she grew older, it seemed that she and her mother just could not get along and were in constant conflict. This made things very difficult for Fatoumatou. Her father decided that the best way to resolve the issue was to send her out to milk the cows and get her away from the house. From that time on, milking the cows became her responsibility.

Milking the cows was not an easy chore, as there were many cows to be milked. The upside of the situation was that her father worked nearby, and this allowed her to spend more time with him. Her father always seemed to find time to listen to her, and that made her feel valued.

One day, while milking the cows, Fatoumatou looked up from her chores and saw Blemou and Vassi Fangamou coming toward the hut. They had come from their home in Bambadinga, a stone's throw away from Bafada. They were dressed in their best clothing, and she knew immediately why they had come.

When her mother called for her, she reluctantly joined them in the hut. She took a place by her mother's side and listened to her father and Blemou speak.

"Blema has worked hard," Blemou declared proudly, "and he is now ready to take a wife."

Fatoumatou felt her face go flush at the announcement. She tried to force a smile, but it wouldn't come. She had always known that this time was imminent, but she didn't feel ready for it. At fifteen, she felt like a little girl that was being pushed through the gates of adulthood, and she fought to understand her own confused emotions.

Blemou took out a small bundle and presented it to her father. Mamadou took it and carefully unfolded the cloth to find a gift of ten cola nuts. If her father accepted the gift, he was giving his consent to allow Blema to court her. If for some reason he were to refuse it however, the arrangement that had been made years before would be broken.

"Thank you, Blemou," her father said. "We will accept this gift as a token of honor and friendship. You have a good son, and he will make a good husband for our daughter."

Blema came to call upon Fatoumatou the next day. The courtship was short and consisted of long walks on endless dirt roads and meals shared with the family. Soon a date was set for the marriage.

There was a time in West African history when a Mandinka would not have married a Fula. In fact, they were bitter enemies. Fatoumatou's father had once told her the story of how, decades earlier, their tribe was forced to flee their lands under the attack of an enemy tribe. With nowhere to run, the Fulas took refuge in Mandinka territory. Showing compassion for the desperate Fula tribe, the Mandinkas allowed them to claim the unused lands around them.

As the Fulas settled in, they soon became more numerous than the Mandinkas. Feeling threatened by the Fula's ever swelling numbers and political differences, the Mandinkas waged war against them, but in the end, the Fulas overcame the Mandinkas and became the dominant tribe. Both tribes were left with bitter feelings after the war, but in the course of time, differences were put aside and civility was restored between them. Eventually, intermarriage became acceptable, opening a door for Blema and Fatoumatou.

Blemou and Vassi were pleased for the children. The next time they came to Mamadou's door they were bearing gifts of colorful fabrics that would be used to make beautiful lapas for the marriage celebration. Blemou presented Mamadou with a bag containing an undisclosed amount of money.

As they discussed plans for the marriage celebration, Mamadou was insistent that it would be done following Muslim tradition, and Blemou graciously conceded to his wishes.

When the day of the marriage arrived, all were filled with excitement and anticipation—all except for Fatoumatou. She was nervous, almost in tears. She was beautiful nonetheless, dressed in the green-blue lapa her mother had made for the occasion. Her hair had been braided and carefully interwoven with dyed animal hair. Kadiatou had spent hours on it the day before.

The traditional ceremony was to take place in an open area in the center of the village. Family and friends had brought wonderful African dishes they had prepared at home and wine that had been saved for special occasions.

There were to be drums and dancing. Blema was pleased to see that someone had brought a Kora, a twenty-one-string instrument made from half a calabash and covered with cow's hide. The instrument was distinctively Mandinka. The Jalibaa, or spiritual singers, were also to be there to sing their songs of praise.

The celebration began as soon as everyone had gathered. After an hour had gone by, the priest came out into the center of the gathering. Everyone went silent when they saw him. In a loud voice, he declared that Blema and Fatoumatou were now husband and wife, and that was it. There was no formal ceremony, but in the eyes of their family and friends, Blema and Fatoumatou were bound by a sacred bond. Everyone wished them joy, prosperity and many children. It was May 12, 1981.

CHAPTER 4
Caught in the Middle

IT WAS NOW OFFICIAL; BLEMA AND FATOUMATOU WERE HUSBAND AND wife. The morning after the celebration, Blema walked with his new bride to her family's hut to gather her things. When they arrived, the family came out to greet them. Blema stayed outside to talk with the men while Fatoumatou went inside.

Slowly, Fatoumatou bundled her clothing and other belongings together into a worn lapa as her mother and sisters watched. Tears welled up in her eyes.

"You'll have to be strong, Fatoumatou!" her mother scolded. "Now, dry your tears!"

Fatoumatou wiped her tears away with the back of her hand. Kadiatou came and sat next to her, and the sisters embraced as if they would never see each other again.

Mustering up her resolve, Fatoumatou finished packing her things, then stood, placed the bundle on her head, and walked outside where her father waited for her.

"Fatoumatou!" Mamadou's face lit up when he saw his daughter. Fatoumatou knew she would miss the warmth of her father's smile. "It looks like Blema is taking my daughter away from me!" he teased.

Fatoumatou gave her father a weak smile.

"Matou. Remember to honor your husband. When you do this, you will bring honor to yourself and to Allah."

"Yes, Papa," she answered, avoiding eye contact. She didn't know how she could bear the thought of leaving him. He had been her rock, and she knew she would feel lost without him.

As if reading her thoughts, Mamadou pulled her close and held her against him. "Everything will be all right, Fatoumatou. You will see. You go be with your husband."

Blema smiled, thankful for the confidence Mamadou had placed in him. He reached out and took a bundle from Fatoumatou, and the two of them began walking toward the road.

Like most young married couples in Guinea-Bissau, he and Fatoumatou would start out their lives together in a small hut next to his parents. Fatoumatou was now considered to be a daughter to his family.

As Blema and Fatoumatou approached the hut, Blemou and Vassi saw them coming and came out to greet them. Vassi came running toward them, her arms stretched wide, and she smiled broadly.

"Welcome, Fatoumatou!" she greeted warmly. "Welcome, both of you! I'm so happy you've finally come."

Blema smiled. "Thank you, Mother."

"This will be the beginning of many happy days together!" Vassi exclaimed.

Suddenly, all of the anxiety that Fatoumatou had felt about coming into a new family suddenly melted away as she was swept into Vassi's warm embrace.

"Thank you," she said. "I know it will."

Blemou took Fatoumatou's things that she had set by her feet, and carried them inside the small hut. Fatoumatou followed behind him.

"We're simple people," Blemou told Fatoumatou as they walked. "But we're happy. You're a welcome addition to our family."

"And you are kind," Fatoumatou replied. "Thank you for everything. I'm sure everything will be fine."

The warm reception that Fatoumatou had received from Blema's family was deeply appreciated. Their kindness and acceptance would help temper the painful days when she yearned for home.

Fatoumatou liked Blema's father, but it was with his mother that she came to have a special bond. Vassi had taken her in from the start and loved her as one of her own. The women cooked together, cleaned together, gardened, talked, laughed, and shared their thoughts and feelings. Vassi taught Fatoumatou the skills of running a household and caring for a family. Fatoumatou learned how to receive guests to make them feel welcome. In many ways, Vassi was more like a mother to her than her own mother had been.

Blema loved to watch these two women as they worked. It made him happy to see them getting along so well. He was proud of his new wife, and he looked forward to building a life with her. Their lives, it seemed, were filled with hope and promise. They could not have foreseen the trouble that lay ahead.

* * * * *

There was a dark cloud, it seemed, which hung over Guinea-Bissau and overshadowed the land with uncertainty. This ominous cloud was one that had shrouded the country for centuries. In fact, no one could remember a time when there had been peace. It had rolled in when the Portuguese took control in 1446 and had remained for over 500 years while the country was ruled by violence and oppression.

In 1956, with hopes of gaining independence from the Portuguese, the African Party for Independence of Guinea and Cape Verde (PAIGC) had been organized. Five years later, an armed rebellion was started against the Portuguese. It took nearly thirteen years of fighting before Guinea-Bissau finally won their independence on September 24, 1973.[3]

Sadly, the end of the war did not bring an end to violence. Local soldiers who had fought along with the Portuguese army against the PAIGC guerrillas were hunted down and slaughtered by the thousands. Buildings that had been built by the Portuguese were targeted, and many were destroyed. The dark cloud remained.[4]

More recently, in 1980 a political upheaval and military coup had established authoritarian dictator Joao Bernardo ‘Nino” Vieira as president.

On one hand, Vieira seemed to benefit the country by creating a market economy and multi-party system. His regime, however, was characterized by the suppression of any political opposition. Vieira was known as a tyrant, quick to eliminate anyone who stood in his way.

Several coup attempts had been made to unseat him throughout the 1980s and early 1990s, but the attempts failed.[5]

Conflict grew between the government and rebel armies. It created a division in the country and an increasingly dangerous situation for the citizens of Guinea-Bissau. Many people felt that civil war was just around the corner, and they were greatly concerned about their own lives and futures.

Blema and Fatoumatou couldn't help but to be concerned about the situation. They had grown up well-acquainted with the horrors that war can bring, and they wanted to see the conflicts come to an end. At the same time, they felt powerless to do anything about it, so amidst the turmoil that surrounded them, they did their best to simply go on with their lives.

* * * * *

"Blema, I need to talk to you." Fatoumatou's face looked flush.

"What is it Matou?" Blema was concerned by the unsettled tone of her voice.

Fatoumatou took Blema's hand and led him away from the house so she could talk with him privately.

"Blema, it's been two months since I have had my womanly time. I believe I'm with child." Fatoumatou froze in place, uncertain of how her husband would react to her news.

"Really?" Blema grinned broadly, unable to conceal his excitement over the news. "That's wonderful, Matou!"

The anxiety that Fatoumatou had silently borne for the past few weeks suddenly melted into a flood of emotion, and tears welled up in her eyes. Blema was touched by her sensitivity. He took her in his arms and firmly kissed her mouth.

"You're a good wife, Matou, and you will be a wonderful mother."

"Thank you, Blema. And you'll be good father."

The months of pregnancy passed quickly for Fatoumatou, in spite of some of the typical challenges. Before she knew it, the time had come for her to deliver. It was late afternoon when her water broke, and by nightfall, she was in full labor.

The timing was good. Just days before, Fatoumatou and Vassi had prepared the hut for the birth. There was never a question as to where the child would be born. It would have been a rare luxury to deliver the baby at the hospital, one that few could afford, and Fatoumatou had never considered it.

Fatoumatou was not concerned, however. With Vassi by her side, she felt that she had nothing to worry about. Vassi had been a midwife for years and seemed to possess a special gift when it came to delivering babies. Fatoumatou knew she was in good hands.

When Vassi learned that Fatoumatou's water had broken, she ushered her to the bed of fresh dry leaves that they had prepared. She brought out strips of cloth that she and Fatoumatou had torn and had set aside. They would need water, and she had sent Blema out to get it. Everything else was ready.

Hours passed as Fatoumatou endured wave after wave of intermittent pain. Blema knelt by near her side, trying to console her as she cried and groaned in distress, but nothing he said or did seemed to help.

"What can I do, Mother?" he asked in frustration.

Vassi's face was calm as she gently wiped Fatoumatou's sweaty arms, legs, and face with a cool, wet cloth.

It was clear to Blema that his mother was now in her element. He knew that there wasn't anything in the world that could bring her more joy and pride than helping to bring a child into the world, especially when the baby was a grandchild. If she felt anxiety or concern about the birth, she didn't show it, and this helped put him at ease.

"Well," Vassi teased, "the best thing that you can do is get out of the way!" Although it had been said in a tone of jest, Blema felt that she had meant it, and he quietly slipped out of the hut.

At the final push, Fatoumatou's hard work was at last rewarded by the strong cry of her newborn son. Exhausted, yet elated, she held her baby in her arms for the very first time. Vassi had cleaned both mother and baby before she called Blema back in to join them.

Blema entered the hut timidly. Fatoumatou noticed him enter and looked up at him, smiling proudly. "It's a boy!" she exclaimed.

Blema came close and touched the boy's face. He was perfect; a plump, dark, and bald miracle.

Blema and Fatoumatou named their son Kamonan, a strong family name. He had been born on May 20, 1982, a date that would never be written down or celebrated. This would ensure him protection from curses or jinxes that might be conjured against him by ill-intended foes.

Two years later, Kamonan was joined by a brother, Sekouna, who was born on March 25, 1984.

In the years to follow, they welcomed Joseph on December 1, 1988; Oldpa on January 2, 1990; and Mousa on September 1, 1991.

After their fifth son was born, Blema and Fatoumatou were resigned to believe they would only have sons. On November 1, 1993, however, they were surprised to receive a baby girl. They named her Bangama. She was bald and beautiful, endowed with a sweet disposition from the start. Not only would Bangama have her parents to watch over her, she was under the mighty protection of her older brothers.

Blema and Fatoumatou loved each of their children, and they felt blessed to have a large family.

* * * * *

Blema's work in the pharmacy had given him a great sense of satisfaction as he gave service to the community, providing medication that was so desperately needed. He and Kounan had seen the business go through many ups and downs, but in the end, the business had held its own and served them well over the years. He was thankful that he had listened to his brother sixteen years before.

Short of being certified to dispense the medications, Blema had learned all aspects of running the business. When he told Kounan of his desire to go to school to become a Certified Pharmaceutical Technician, his brother was supportive and encouraged him to go.

Blema soon enrolled at the Ecole de Pharmacie de Dunka in Guinea-Bissau. He attended school at night so he could continue working in the pharmacy during the daytime.

After nearly a year, Blema walked into the pharmacy one day to find that his brother had not come in to work. This was the third day in a row that Kounan had not been there. It was unlike him to stay away for any reason, so when he didn't come in, Blema knew there was cause to worry.

"Maneh, I'd like for you to watch the store for a while," said Blema. "I'm going to go check on Kounan."

Blema ran all the way to Kounan's house. When he arrived, he found him lying on the bed, delirious with fever.

Kounan's wife, Vassi, was hovering over him. The deep lines of worry engraved on her forehead and the puffiness around her eyes revealed that she had not slept for some time. Always ministering to the needs of others, Vassi reminded Blema of his mother, and he guessed that it wasn't by chance that the women shared the same name.

"How is he?" he asked.

Vassi looked at Blema with a look of deep concern. "Not well," she answered.

Blema stepped past her and knelt down on the ground next to his brother. "Kounan, I'm here," he said gently. Kounan gave no indication that he had heard him.

"I'm sorry you're sick, brother," he went on. "I'm here to help you."

Just then, Kounan jerked forward and vomited upon the ground. Blema stepped back, but it was too late. His shirt was soiled, along with everything around him. Vassi jumped up to clean up the mess.

"This is really serious, Vassi." Blema told her. "Kounan is going to need medication immediately."

"What do think is wrong with him?"

"I don't know for sure, but I'm worried he might have malaria. A lot of people are suffering with it right now, so I'm afraid the medication will be hard to find. If you'll stay here with him, I'll go see what I can do."

"Of course," she said without any intention of leaving Kounan's side.

Blema moved quickly. "Pray for me, Vassi." he said as he left the hut.

Blema returned hours later, exhausted, but pleased that he had been able to obtain the medication. When he entered the hut, several women had gathered around Kounan, washing him down with cool, wet cloths, rubbing his skin with herbs, and making sure he was comfortable.

Blema approached Kounan and helped him take the medication. Kounan had become weak, and it was with great effort that he drank the thick liquid.

Hours passed by, but Kounan didn't seem to respond to the medication. Kounan's family stayed by his side and continued to watch over him, but, in spite of the medication and the attentive care, Kounan's condition grew worse, and by the next day, he was dead.

Blema was heartsick. Kounan had been more like a father to him than a brother, and he loved him dearly. Suddenly he felt lost.

Blema's father came to him and reminded him that with Kounan's death, there would changes in the family. First of all, there would be a shift in family status. Now, Blema would be considered the oldest son. Blema's father also reminded him that along with the title came a greater level of family responsibility. Since Vassi and her children had been left without financial support, there was an expectation that he would marry her and help raise his brother's children.

Blema had never taken responsibility lightly, but the decision to marry Kounan's wife was not a simple one. He and Fatoumatou had been married for sixteen years, and they had six children to raise. Feeling that Fatoumatou was not going to happily accept the idea, he dreaded having to talk to her about it. When he finally brought up the matter, he was not prepared for her intense response.

"If you marry Vassi," Fatoumatou cried with anguish and her voice tight with emotion, "it will tear our family apart!"

Having been raised in a polygamous household, Fatoumatou had witnessed the complicated dynamics that often accompany the arrangement, and she wanted no part of it. Blema understood Fatoumatou's feelings, and he reassured her that he would honor them.

Although Blema did not marry Vassi, he committed to help them financially whenever he could out of compassion for her and her children.

Since Kounan's death, there were also important decisions to be made concerning the pharmacy. Kounan had owned and managed the business for many years. Now it would be up to Blema to either take over the pharmacy or sell it. This would not be an easy decision. It would be hard to fill his brother's shoes. Not knowing what to do, Blema went to his knees and asked God for direction.

In the end, he decided to keep the pharmacy. Although the prospect of running the business frightened him, he knew that if he gave it his best, God would sustain him in his decision.

The transition seemed difficult in the beginning, but Blema was determined to see it through. Because he had completed only one year of a two-year pharmaceutical program and had not yet received his certificate, he was unable to legally dispense the medications. It was necessary for him to retain the employees who had worked for his brother in order to keep the business open. The employees agreed to stay on and over time, things seemed to fall into place.

The business grew, and by 1998, Blema had become respected in the community as a business owner. Blema and Fatoumatou enjoyed the monetary rewards of owning a business, and eventually they moved their family into a home closer to town. Their new house was larger and more modern, with divided rooms and a bathroom. It had access to power and had been hooked up to water, but the water system was not reliable and they still had to bring water in from the well.

The house had a kitchen, but because there were no kitchen appliances, the cooking had to be done outside. Still, the house was a great improvement over the village huts that they had been living in, and Blema and Fatoumatou were happy and content.

Unfortunately, the dark clouds of Guinea-Bissau were gathering once again.

* * * * *

In 1994, Guinea-Bissau had held its first free election since gaining independence. To the surprise of many, and in spite of fierce opposition, Joao Bernardo 'Nino" Vieira had been elected president. The group of rebels that had orchestrated previous coup attempts against him had reorganized after the election, and the already tense political climate escalated.

It was now 1998, and civil war between the government officials and the rebel faction seemed imminent. As political tensions heated up, the situation began to threaten everything that was important to Blema and his family—their home, business, and way of life.

Although Blema had no desire to get involved politically, the time had come when he felt that he could no longer stand back and hope that things would get better. He joined up with the Organisation de Societe Civil (OSC), a non-violent citizen's organization that had been formed to protect citizen's rights, hoping to assist them to foster compromise between the warring factions to avoid civil war.

Blema soon became a leader within the organization. As he met with the other leaders to discuss the country's issues, they all agreed that the only way the opposing parties would ever work out their differences would be through opening up communication between them. To encourage them to come together and talk, they planned to arrange a meeting between the government officials and leaders of the opposing faction. Through offering an opportunity to discuss their issues openly, they hoped to provide a catalyst for better understanding and eventual peace.

To their great satisfaction, the arrangement was accepted by both parties, and a meeting was scheduled for June.

When the day of the meeting finally arrived, Blema met early with the other OSC representatives so they could all go together. He had been asked to be present at the meeting along with them. His role was well defined. He was to listen to the discussions while maintaining a position of neutrality and to act as a mediator for the two opposing sides when necessary.

After this intense briefing, the group of a dozen men made their way to the government building where the meeting would be held. As Blema entered the building, he could feel the thick tension in the air. He quietly took his place beside the others and watched as the discussions commenced.

Despite the tense climate, the meeting opened in an impressively orderly manner. Unfortunately, it did not take long for the tides to change. Anger soon flared on both sides, and the talks turned into an intense argument. With neither side willing to bend, the meeting quickly got out of hand.

Some of the OSC representatives, forgetting why they had come, chose sides and became involved in the arguments. Blema was determined to stay true to his assignment. He tried to maintain a position of neutrality and diplomacy and to bring order back to the meeting, but in spite of his best efforts, he found himself caught in the middle of the hot debate. The discussions could not be brought to order and were eventually suspended.

Blema's noble attempts had not only been disregarded, they had backfired. When everything was over, he found himself accused by government leaders of sympathizing with the rebels. As he prepared to leave, he looked across the room and noticed one of the government officials glaring at him. The look went right through him, and he left the meeting fearing the consequences.

Days later, the word had spread that Vieira was sending soldiers out to eliminate anyone found supporting the rebels. Knowing that he had been unfairly marked as a rebel sympathizer, Blema felt vulnerable.

Over the next few weeks he did not let his guard down. During the daytime he tried to stay apprised of what was happening around him while he worked at the pharmacy, and at night, he slept away from his family as not to put them in danger.

As tension between the factions continued to increase, violent outbreaks became more frequent. The situation had divided the country; brother had turned against brother and friend against friend until Blema didn't know where he could turn or whom he could trust.

In mid-afternoon on November 23, 1998, Blema looked up from his work to notice soldiers approaching his pharmacy. They were led by his good friend, Captain Carlos Sanha, who had become a government soldier. Blema and Carlos had been friends for as long as he could remember, and he trusted him like a brother. He was surprised and confused when he saw him enter the pharmacy. He tried to appeal to the sensitivities of his friend and hoped that their friendship would outweigh any government army imposed command, but it wasn't to be.

A brutal attack by the soldiers had forced him to flee his home, family, country, everything he loved in an attempt to preserve his life and the lives of his family. The separation from his family had left him devastated.

Now, after eight months on the run, Blema was worn down. The journey had taken a toll on him, physically and emotionally, and it had taken everything within him just to survive. Even his appearance had changed. His skin had become hard and leathery from exposure to the elements, and he had lost enough weight to make his ribs stick out when he took off his shirt. The dust and the dirt had discolored his skin, and his hair had become long and matted.

Blema's emotions, once sure and steady, had become fragile and remained close to the surface, adding unbearable weight to the journey. There were times when he felt numb to any emotion at all, and in a strange way, this seemed to offer respite for a time. But inevitably, the heartache always returned, seizing him with the same terrible intensity that he had felt right after the attack, making the pain caused by blisters, scrapes, mosquito bites, swollen ankles, and sore muscles seem insignificant. He had come to feel almost subhuman—animal-like—and it had become a daily mental exercise just to keep his mind straight. He missed his family more than he ever thought possible.

Overcome at times by his own troubled emotions, it was all that he could do to continue on. Now, more than ever, he found himself searching for God. He refused to abandon his prayers, even though he felt at times that God had abandoned him. In his darkest hours, he turned to him for help, having nowhere else to go.

Ironically, it was during these most desperate, lonely times that he often felt a strong impression that he was being watched over, and somehow, in this lost and lonely state, he knew he wasn't alone. It was this feeling, this hope, that kept him moving forward . . . believing.

CHAPTER 5
Precious Birth

FATOUMATOU WAS SURE THAT THERE WAS NO WAY SHE COULD EVER repay Kadiatou and Therno for the help and support that they had given to her during her desperate time of need. It had touched her deeply to see how they had unselfishly opened up their home to her family. They had watched over her children for nearly three months while she was in the hospital, and then for another three months as she convalesced in their home. She didn't know what she would have ever done without them.

Fatoumatou had always felt close to Kadiatou from the time they were little girls. Now, after so much had happened, the love she felt for her sister was deeper and meant more than it ever had before.

As the older sister, Fatoumatou had always looked out for Kadiatou and protected her. Now, it seemed that the roles had been reversed, and it was she who leaned on Kadiatou's strength. It was a comfort to have her near.

It was now January, and Fatoumatou was coming to the end of a difficult pregnancy. Having not fully recovered from her illness, she hoped that she would have the strength she needed to give birth. Kadiatou had reassured her that things would be fine and promised that she would not leave her side when it was time for her to deliver the child.

Kadiatou was true to her promise. After a long, difficult labor, Fatoumatou gave birth to a baby boy. She named the child Djabril, which is Gabriel in English. He was small but beautiful. Djabril's tiny head was crowned with soft, curly black hair, and his tender, reddish-brown skin seemed to glisten in the light of the day. Kadiatou had wrapped him up in a clean, white cloth and placed him near Fatoumatou's side where he slept peacefully.

Fatoumatou loved this little boy from the very first moment she held him in her arms, but his birth had been bittersweet. It grieved her to know that Blema would never see him, and that the child would never know his father. Her heart ached for them both.

Djabril's birth had been extremely hard on Fatoumatou. It had left her feeling wrung out and weak. Soon after the birth, she began to feel shooting pains in her abdomen and then began to hemorrhage.

Therno rushed her to the hospital once again, but the hospital refused to admit her. She was turned away because her first visit had not been paid for. Frightened by her unstable condition, Therno brought her back to their home, where Kadiatou took over her care once again.

Kadiatou did everything she could to help her older sister. She gathered healing herbs and then administered them in the way her mother had taught her. She prayed and hoped that her efforts would stop the bleeding and ease Fatoumatou's pain. To her great relief, the remedies seemed to work, and in time, the bleeding stopped.

Still, it would be nearly a year before Fatoumatou's body had fully recovered and her strength had returned. She felt immensely grateful for all that Kadiatou had done for her, and she thanked the Lord for sparing her life once again.

CHAPTER 6
Benin

By August of 2000, Blema had finally arrived in Benin and stood in line outside of the United Nations High Commissioner for Refugees (UNHCR) office near the Kpomasse refugee camp. After he had made his way to the front of the line, he entered the office and presented himself to the official, expecting to be directed to the camp.

"What's your name?" the official questioned.

"Blema Fangamou."

"Can you read and write?"

"Yes, sir."

"Then take this form and fill it out. Write down as much information as you can."

"How long will it be before I can I get into the camp?"

"What? Take a look in back of you, man. All of these people are waiting to get in. You'll have to go through the same process as everyone else. You can't get into the camp until you've been approved by the UNHCR and obtain refugee status, and that could take time."

"How long?"

"Who knows? Some of these people have been waiting for months. Just fill out the form and we'll put it on file with the others. Now, move aside, you're holding up the line."

It didn't take long for Blema to fill out the form, and then he returned it to the official.

It was dusk by the time he joined the mass of bodies outside, and with his piece of cardboard, he claimed an open space where he could bed down for the night.

"Hello." Blema said casually to a man who sat eating a piece dried fish. The man acknowledged him with a nod.

"So . . . how are you getting by?" asked Blema.

"All right," replied the man.

"No, I mean, how are you getting food? Is there any work around here?"

"Not much. There's a local construction company that comes to the office every morning to hire day laborers. If you're lucky, you might be able to get work with them. If not, you'll be begging from the lucky ones. Sometimes, those who work will share what they have, but for the most part, it's every man for himself."

By six o'clock the next morning, Blema was up and had joined the others as they waited for the supervisor of the construction company to show up. When the supervisor arrived, he began pointing out his crew, but he looked past Blema as if he wasn't there. This happened for several days in a row.

Not willing to give in to discouragement, Blema continued to show up at the office every day until finally, he was given a job.

As part of the crew, Blema worked long, hard hours doing a variety of jobs. He did everything he was asked to do, knowing that if he let his work slip, there were men waiting in line to take his place.

The work was physically exhausting and the pay was next to nothing, but the money he earned allowed him to take care of his basic needs, and it gave him a sense of normalcy, which he was grateful for.

* * * * *

Blema had been wearing the same clothing he had worn for months. His shirt had become tattered and his pants were worn thin. After working for the construction company for several weeks, he decided that it was time to buy some desperately needed new clothing, so on a day when he wasn't working, he set out for the market in Tokpa, several miles away.

Following the dirt road to Tokpa, Blema walked until he could see the little village market ahead. He had passed only a few people along the way, but as he neared the market, more and more people occupied the street. As people bustled around him, he looked up and saw someone he recognized. The man's name was Lamani.

Blema had known Lamani for years. He was a salesman who traveled all over West Africa, selling rice, flour, shoes, clothing, and jewelry. He had occasionally come into Blema's pharmacy in Guinea-Bissau. His home was in Salikenhe, not far from where Therno and Kadiatou lived. Lamani knew Therno and Kadiatou well, and they had become good friends.

"Lamani!" Blema called out. Lamani turned back at the sound of his name.

"How do you know my name?" he asked, not recognizing Blema.

"It's me, Lamani! Blema. Blema Fangamou."

"You can't be Blema. Blema's dead."

"Lamani, I am not dead. Look at me. Do I look dead to you?"

"No, you don't look dead, but you don't look like Blema Fangamou."

"Well, I *am* Blema Fangamou, and I'm *not* dead!"

Blema just stood, looking into Lamani's eyes until suddenly, Lamani was hit with a flash of recognition.

"Blema, I can't believe it's you! Everyone thinks you're dead. Fatoumatou told me that you had been killed by soldiers."

"Fatoumatou? You've seen Fatoumatou? Where is she?"

"She's in Salikenhe with her sister, Kadiatou. I just saw her a few weeks ago."

"Are the children with her?"

"Yes. I guess they've been there for quite some time."

"How are they? Are they all right?"

"They seem to be. Fatoumatou was very sick for a while, but she seems to be doing better. I guess the baby's birth was really hard on her."

"The baby?"

"Oh, I'm sorry, I guess there was no way for you to know. She had a little boy. I can't remember what she named him, but he's a cute little guy."

"Oh my. That's wonderful. I just feel sorry that I couldn't be there for her."

"I heard what happened to you in Guinea-Bissau. That's too bad, man. I can see that it's been really hard on you."

"Yes, it has been."

"So, what are you going to do now, Blema? Are you going back to Senegal?"

"No, I can't. Not yet anyway. Do you remember Maneh, my employee at the pharmacy?"

"Yes."

"They killed him, Lamani! I read it in a newspaper the other day. If I went back now, they would do the same to me. My family is safer right now without me."

"Man, what a bad situation!"

"I'm waiting for my refugee status to come through. If I can get into the refugee camp, I'll be able to stay there until things calm down. Are you going back to Senegal soon?"

"Yes, I'm going back tomorrow."

"Good. Will you do me a favor? If you see Fatoumatou, will you tell her where I am and that I am all right? Tell her I'll come to her as soon as it's safe. And will you tell her that I love her?"

"Sure, Blema. You know, for a dead man you have a lot to say!"

Blema laughed. He couldn't remember the last time he had laughed.

"Thanks, Lamani. God bless you."

"You too, Blema. It was good to see you."

"And you. Take care and travel safe."

CHAPTER 7
Searching for Blema

"I'm sorry, Lamani," Fatoumatou insisted, "Blema is dead!"

"No, Fatoumatou, I've seen him."

"Lamani, I know you mean well, but it's been a long time. You must have seen someone who looks like Blema."

"No, Fatoumatou, listen to me. I know it was Blema. I've seen him. I've talked with him. I told him that you are here and that you and the children are well and safe. He wanted me to tell you that he is alive and that he misses you. He hopes to come to you when it is safe, but wants you to understand that if he were to come back now, he would be putting all of you in danger. He can't come back until things calm down. He'll come for you as soon as he can."

Fatoumatou went silent. For nearly a year and a half she had believed that Blema was dead. She had not considered the possibility that her husband might have survived the attack. A wave of emotion washed over her as the thoughts and questions came racing into her mind. Suddenly she went into a panic.

"I need to go to him, Lamani!"

"What?"

"I need to go find him. If I don't do it now, I'll lose track of him. I may never see him again."

Lamani could see the distress in her face. "It's a bad situation, I know, Fatoumatou. But you can't go to him. The journey is just too hard. It would eat you alive. You're better off to stay here and wait for Blema to come to you. He loves you and the children, and you know he'll come for you when it's safe."

"But that could be too late! With all the trouble around us, anything could happen. If I go and find him now, we can find a safe place. As long as we're together, we can build our lives over somewhere else. If I wait, there's no telling what might happen."

Kadiatou had stepped outside and overheard part of the conversation. Although she didn't want to intrude, she felt like she needed to speak up.

"Fatoumatou, you need to listen to Lamani. He's right. It would be very difficult for you to travel that far. And even if you were able to, it would be nearly impossible for you to find Blema. It would be best for you to wait for him."

"I can't do that, Kadiatou! I understand your concern, but I just know that if I don't go now, I'll lose him forever. I've lost him once; I can't take the chance of losing him again."

Fatoumatou's face had become twisted with anxiety, and tears welled in the corner of her eyes. Kadiatou looked at her sister pitifully as she realized that all of the talk in the world would not persuade her to stay.

Kadiatou looked over to Therno who had joined them. He shrugged his shoulders as if to answer his wife's unspoken question, "What do we do?"

"What about the children, Fatoumatou?" Kadiatou asked. "They won't survive that long of a journey. You can't put them through that again."

Fatoumatou thought back to what the children had endured on the last journey, and knew her sister was right. After a moment of silence, she bowed her head in defeat as the tears began to flow.

Kadiatou looked to Therno once again. He seemed to be in deep thought. He looked to see his wife gazing at him. The look on her face was one that he knew all too well. Sensing what she was about to do, he shook his head, somewhat amused by her predictability. He knew it was pointless to try to talk her out of it and nodded his head in approval.

Kadiatou moved closer to Fatoumatou, putting her arm around her shoulder. "Fatoumatou, we know this is important to you and we want to help you. You know we can't keep Djabril. He's still breastfeeding and needs his mother, but you can leave the other children with us while you travel. You'll be able to travel much more quickly that way."

"We've saved some money," added Therno. "Enough to purchase a train ticket to Mali. I know that's only a portion of the journey, but at least it will help."

Fatoumatou smiled at Therno and then turned to Kadiatou wrapping both arms around her neck. "Oh, thank you!" she said sincerely. "Thank you, Therno. Thank you, both!"

She then turned to Lamani, who had been quietly listening to the conversation. "And thank you, Lamani. You are a good man."

"You know I'd go with you if I could," Lamani said apologetically, "but I've been away from my family for a long time. They need me here."

"Yes, I know. It's going to be all right. The Lord will go with me." Fatoumatou took his hand and squeezed it. "It will be all right, you'll see."

Within days, Fatoumatou had made the arrangements to leave. On the morning of her departure, she made a bundle with some bread and cheese and a change of clothing for the journey and set it by the door. The children came and flocked around her. Bangama grabbed her leg as though she wouldn't let it go.

Fatoumatou bent down where she could look each of her children in the eyes. This was one of the most difficult things she had ever done. If it were not for her belief that she was doing what would ultimately be best for her family, she would have found it impossible to leave her children.

"How long are you going to be gone?" asked Mousa.

"It's going to seem like a long time," Fatoumatou answered, "but I'll go and find your father and we'll come back as quickly as we can, I promise you. Therno and Kadiatou will watch over you while I'm gone and make sure you have what you need. You mind them and do everything they tell you to do. Do you understand?" The children nodded their heads in unison.

"When you see Father," said Joseph, "will you tell him that we love him and that we're waiting for him."

"I will, Joseph," replied Fatoumatou. "Since you're one of the oldest, you'll need to help watch over your brothers and sister. Therno and Kadiatou are depending on you."

"Yes, Mother."

Fatoumatou embraced each of the children before turning to leave. She felt a sudden tug of self-doubt and wondered if she were doing the right thing. She offered up a silent prayer, picked up Djabril, and headed in the direction of the train station.

Boarding the train with her baby carefully bound in a bundle against her chest, she sat on a seat beside the window so she could watch as the miles passed by. The rocking motion and rhythmic sound of the trains clanking wheels lulled her baby to sleep.

Time passed slowly, and by the time they had arrived in Mali, the baby was awake and crying. It was hot inside the train, and his little body was sticky with sweat. He was hungry, and as much as Fatoumatou tried, he would not be comforted. Fatoumatou understood the baby's outburst. She felt close to one herself. She too was hungry, hot, and spent from the travel.

Therno had instructed her before she left to find a Catholic church when she reached Mali. There, she was told, she would find a meal and a place to sleep. When she got off the train, she asked directions from the locals and then walked through the streets until she found the Catholic church.

As she climbed up the steps to the church, she was greeted by a robust woman with an angelic smile who welcomed her and brought her inside. The woman led her to a dining area that was filled with people who appeared to be just as worn as she. Some were standing in a line with bowls in hand, while others sat and ate.

The smell of soup and rice filled the room. Fatoumatou filled a bowl and ate until she was satisfied. After she had finished, the angel woman led her to a large room where bamboo mats were spread out from wall to wall on the floor. "You can rest here," the woman said.

Fatoumatou thanked her for her kindness and dropped down on a mat next to the wall.

As she lay on the mat nursing Djabril, she quietly sang him a Fula lullaby until the two of them drifted off into a deep sleep. When morning came, she gathered her things, picked up Djabril, and was ready to be on her way.

On her way out, Fatoumatou was given a small bundle of food and the bus fare to the next town, both for which she was most grateful. The bus station was close by, and she knew that if she hurried, she could catch the early bus.

Arriving barely on time, Fatoumatou boarded the bus and took a seat near the back with Djabril perched on her lap. The bus made frequent stops, and before long, there was standing room only. The travelers were packed tightly in the isles with no breathing room between them. Fatoumatou felt like she was being suffocated. By the time she had reached her destination, she was looking forward to continuing her journey on foot.

When the bus made it's final stop, Fatoumatou got out and began walking. She felt hungry and pulled out the food she was given at the church. Although she had tried to be careful to ration the food, there was now only a small piece of bread and a carrot left in her depleted bundle. Still, she knew that she had to push on.

In the days that followed, food became a constant concern. Fatoumatou was never quite sure where her next meal would come from. As she walked, if she were near a populated area, she depended on the sympathies of strangers. When she was in the countryside, she gleaned the fields for root vegetables. Still, it was never enough, and she constantly felt the gnawing pangs of hunger. She worried about Djabril. She knew he was not getting enough milk, and it frightened her. The sound of his cries pierced her motherly heart like a dagger.

As the days wore on, Fatoumatou did the best she could to care for Djabril and put as many miles behind her as possible. Some days were better than others. She had been able to walk over twenty miles in a day, but had struggled to make three the next. The important thing, she decided, was to keep on going.

Most of her travels were done in the daylight when she felt safe. Although she looked forward to getting off of her feet at night, it was usually a challenge to find a place to sleep.

On most nights she ended up in the bushes, but there were always swarms of hungry mosquitoes waiting for her there. She tried to protect Djabril from the insects by wrapping him in her lapa, sacrificing her own skin to their bites, but the mosquitoes seemed to have an appetite for Djabril's tender skin and they made a meal of him through the lapa.

Sometimes, when she was lucky, she would find a car along the way that had not been locked up and climbed into the back seat to sleep. She was not the only one who had this idea. At times, four or five people were packed in a car.

Within the first weeks of travel, the toils of the journey had already taken a toll on Fatoumatou as she fought hunger, thirst, lack of sleep, and exposure to the sun. With no place to bathe or wash her hair or clothes, she began to take on the appearance of something wild, and it became increasingly difficult to get a handout. When she approached people for food, they thought she was crazy and went out of their way to avoid her. Sometimes she felt as if she *were* crazy. Even though she was surrounded by people, she felt alone, and in time, she succumbed to an acute sense of loneliness and depression.

The journey had become more difficult than she had ever imagined it would be. The tremendous weight from the hardship bore down heavily upon her, and it became almost unbearable.

After traveling for several weeks, she found herself walking one day along a dusty road which lay somewhere out in the middle of nowhere. Having become physically and emotionally spent, she stopped in the middle of the road and slumped to the ground. As she looked at the road ahead of her, the scene became distorted by a warm flood of tears that suddenly filled her eyes, and she wondered how she would go on. Holding Djabril tightly against her breast, she rocked him back and forth and sobbed without reservation.

It was hard to explain, even to herself, what had brought her here. The love that she felt for Blema and her children was deep, but only now did she realize how deep. She had been willing to sacrifice everything, even putting her own life at risk, to be with him again. Somehow, this sacrifice had only increased her love, making it feel sacred. She wanted to believe that she would find him again, and that everything was going to work out, but that was becoming increasingly hard to do.

She did not doubt that God was near, helping her. Having become a Christian soon after marrying Blema, she had come to lean on her faith. She had no doubt that her Savior was mindful of her and would support her in all her trials. He had given her strength beyond her own, and she knew it. Still, it was difficult to avoid the disturbing thoughts that floated around in her mind, testing her faith.

"What if I'm unable to find the strength to keep going?" she wondered. "What if Djabril is unable to bear up, and I lose him? What if I'm unable to find Blema when I get to Benin? What if, for some reason, I'm not able to return to my children?"

It was easy to become overwhelmed by these thoughts, and it took all that was in her to fight them away. She knew that if she were going to survive, she would have to put her trust in God and keep on going.

Fatoumatou cried until her tears were spent. Gathering her strength once again, she stood, brushed herself off, and continued down the road.

* * * * *

Treading slowly across West Africa, Fatoumatou had unknowingly taken the same route that Blema had taken months before. After nearly six months of travel, she finally arrived in Cotonau, the capital city of Benin.

It was dusk by the time she entered the streets of the city, and being close to exhaustion, she searched for a place she could settle for the night. As she walked, she noticed an armed security guard pacing in front of the businesses that lined the street, and she decided that this would be the safest place for her to sleep. The guard paid little attention to her the first night, but when she had returned the second night, he approached her to ask what she was doing there.

When Fatoumatou saw him approach, she braced herself for his rebuke.

"Are you all right, lady?" he asked. His gentle voice of concern caught her off guard, and his unexpected kindness made her crumble.

Through her tears, she explained how she had been separated from her husband, and how she had left her children behind in Senegal to come in search for him.

"My baby is sick," she sobbed. "We're hungry, and I don't know what to do."

The guard frowned as he looked down at Fatoumatou and Djabril. Djabril had become weak and frail, and the sight of him filled the guard with pity. Reaching into his pocket, he took out a piece of flat bread and broke off a small piece off the end. He placed it in Djabril's tiny hand, and then handed what remained to Fatoumatou.

"What makes you think that your husband is here in Benin?" he asked.

"Our friend, Lamani, saw him here."

"I see. When did he see him?"

"About six months ago."

"Six months ago!" he exclaimed, shaking his head. "Six months is a long time. He could be anywhere by now. I hate to say this, ma'am, but I'm afraid that your chances of finding him are pretty slim."

"Yes, I know. But I've come this far. I need to try."

"Of course you do. You know, if by any chance he's still here in Benin, he might have gone to the Kpomasse refugee camp. You might try there. If you go to the UNHCR office, they might have a record of him."

"Do you think so? How far is the office?"

"About forty kilometers."

Fatoumatou had traveled nearly three thousand kilometers by then, but at that moment, the thought of traveling another forty kilometers seemed nearly impossible. She felt that it might as well have been a million.

As if reading her thoughts, the guard turned to the street and whistled loudly as a taxi pulled up next to him. Reaching into his pocket once again, the guard pulled out a paper bill and handed it to the driver, giving him instructions to take Fatoumatou and Djabril to the UNHCR office. To Fatoumatou, this man had been a godsend.

"God bless you, sir!" she exclaimed as she and Djabril slipped into the back seat of the taxi.

"And God be with you!" he said.

CHAPTER 8
The Reunion

EDWARD LOOKED UP FROM HIS DESK INSIDE THE UNHCR OFFICE to see Fatoumatou walk through the door with her child, and her disheveled appearance drew his attention.

"What can I do for you, madam?" he asked.

Fatoumatou walked up close to the desk, jostling Djabril nervously on her hip.

"I'm looking for my husband," she said, trying to keep the sound of desperation out of her voice.

"What is your name?"

"Fatoumatou Diallo."

"Is your husband expecting you?"

"No, sir. I was hoping that he had registered here."

"Well, I can check, but do you see these files? It would take me awhile to go through them. What makes you think your husband is here?"

"Our friend saw him here."

"Oh? When was that?"

"It would have been March."

"March? That was a long time ago. Chances are, he's either gone to the refugee camp by now, or he's moved on."

"Would you please check?"

What's his name?"

"Blema . . . Blema Fangamou!"

Edward straightened up. Blema had been coming into the office every morning at six o'clock for months now, and he knew him well. He wasn't about to reveal this to Fatoumatou, however. Not yet.

"Well . . ." he said, "It'll take some time to go through the files. It might be best if you come back in the morning. I'll be here at six o'clock."

"But, I don't mind waiting."

"No, Fatoumatou. You come back in the morning."

Reluctantly, Fatoumatou went away to find a place to bed down for the night.

When she had found a place to sleep and had settled in, it wasn't long before Djabril was sleeping soundly. She tried to sleep too but couldn't. Her thoughts were running wildly through her mind, and as much as she tried, she couldn't shut them down. She worried about what she would do if she didn't find Blema.

As she lay quietly, Fatoumatou began to pray silently. She had left Senegal, trusting that God would lead her to Blema. Now that she had come all this way, she would need nothing less than a miracle. The prayer seemed to quiet her fears, and sometime in the night, she drifted off to sleep.

Without a watch, Fatoumatou didn't know what time it was when she awoke. The sun was just beginning to come up over the horizon when she made her way to the UNHCR office.

When she arrived, a group of men had already gathered just outside the office. As she stood by and watched them approach, she found herself searching each face in hope that she might see Blema. Although she had not expected to see him, she couldn't help feeling let down when she didn't. Soon, Edward appeared at the doorway.

"Good Morning, Fatoumatou," he greeted cheerfully. "It's a beautiful morning."

"Good morning, sir. Yes it is."

"Well, have you found your husband?"

"What? No, sir. Were you able to find his file?"

Edward frowned and shook his head. "No, I'm afraid not."

Fatoumatou's heart sank. It seemed that her fears had just become a reality, and the disappointment was more than she could absorb. She suddenly felt weak.

Edward stepped toward her and took hold of her arm to keep her from falling. He slowly turned her around to face the crowd of men once again.

"I've done better than that, Fatoumatou," he said with a smile.

Edward looked out at the crowd until he had spotted a thin, tired looking man, and he pointed directly at him. "Does that man look familiar to you?" he asked.

Fatoumatou looked at the man but didn't recognize him.

Blema had come to the office that morning just as he did every morning and had been too heavily engaged in conversation to notice Fatoumatou standing just feet away from him. Edward caught his attention when he began pointing at him.

Turning toward Edward, Blema stopped short when he saw Fatoumatou standing next to him. Their eyes met, and suddenly he couldn't breathe.

"BLEMA!" Fatoumatou squealed when she realized the man she had been looking at was her husband.

"Fatoumatou?" Blema answered in disbelief. It had been two long years since he had seen her, and now here she was, holding their son whom he had never seen. He had dreamed of this moment many times but never dared believe it would actually happen.

Blema quickly made his way through the crowd to where they stood. He took Djabril from Fatoumatou's arms and studied his face. Pulling Fatoumatou into a tight embrace, he laughed emotionally as the tears began to flow.

The men that stood nearby watched as the reunion unfolded before them. Touched by the scene, they all broke out into applause. Edward grinned as he stepped toward Blema and slapped his back. "Congratulations, Blema. I'm happy for you."

Blema thought it almost inconceivable that Fatoumatou had come all the way from Senegal to find him. As much it gladdened him to have her there, it broke his heart to imagine all that she and Djabril had been through. It was apparent to him that they were both very sick and would need immediate medical help.

Blema helped Fatoumatou and Djabril find a place to rest while he found them something to eat. He then went back to talk to Edward.

"Edward, I'm really concerned about Fatoumatou and Djabril," he confided.

"I'm already on it, Blema," Edward replied. "I've called the Minister of the Interior and explained the situation. It took some convincing, but they've given permission to send them both to the hospital in Cotonau for treatment. I've made arrangements for transportation."

"I don't know what to say. Thank you, Edward."

"No problem, Blema. You know, being here every day and seeing all the pain and suffering that goes on, it's nice to see a happy ending once in a while. It was my pleasure to do that for you."

"You don't know what that means to me. I really appreciate it."

"The van will be ready to pick up Fatoumatou and Djabril in about an hour. I know that you'll want to go with them, but I think you should stay here."

"Oh? Why?"

"Well, now that Fatoumatou and Djabril are here, I think it that we should review your refugee status. I'd like to see you and your family get into the camp just as soon as Fatoumatou and Djabril get out of the hospital. In order to make that happen, I'll need you here to supply the information we need."

"You've been very good to us Edward. Thanks again. I'll go help Fatoumatou get ready to go."

After searching the records, Edward found the earlier forms that Blema had filled out when he first arrived in Benin. Those forms were updated to include Fatoumatou and Djabril. He then made several phone calls and convinced the Organization of the Union of Africa (OUA) representatives of the urgency of the situation. The case would now be given higher priority.

By late that afternoon, Fatoumatou and Djabril were on their way to the hospital. Two days after that, Blema stood in front of the OUA committee to present them with his forms and an oral testimony. It would be up to the committee to determine if he and his family qualified for refugee status.

Standing before a panel of a half dozen men, Blema proceeded to relay the tragic events that had brought him and his wife to Benin and had separated them from their children. As much as he tried to keep his emotions in check, it had been impossible.

After his emotional testimony, the decision had been unanimous. Blema and Fatoumatou and little Djabril did indeed qualify for refugee status. They were given a certification of notification to present at the Kpomasse refugee camp just as soon as Fatoumatou and Djabril were released from the hospital. The next day, Blema was taken to the hospital where he would join his wife and child.

* * * * *

The Cotonau hospital was one of the best in Benin, yet it had been functioning with limited equipment, supplies, and staff, and it struggled to meet the needs of the people. Although it was far from ideal, it had been months since Fatoumatou had slept on a bed, and to her, it felt like heaven.

Once Blema had arrived, he located the doctor and spoke to him about Fatoumatou and Djabril's condition. He learned that both mother and child had contracted malaria and were being treated for malnutrition. They had been placed a large room and assigned to one of the dozens of single beds that lined the wall.

"Fatoumatou," Blema announced when he saw her. "I have good news!"

"What is it, Blema?"

"We've been granted refugee status!"

"What? Really?"

"Yes. Now when you get out of the hospital, we don't have to worry about having a roof over our heads or wonder where our next meal will come from. We'll have good water to drink, and we'll have medication when we're sick. Things are finally looking up for us, Fatoumatou!"

"Oh . . . that's good, Blema!" said Fatoumatou. It was good to hear her husband's voice and have him close to her again.

"Now, we'll just have to concentrate on getting you two well," he said.

Blema was committed to stay with Fatoumatou and Djabril for as long as it took them to get well. The hospital staff had been kind and understanding, allowing him to sleep in a hospital bed when one was available. Most of the time, however, the beds were full and he ended up sleeping on the floor.

Over the next few weeks, with the help of medication and much needed bed rest, Fatoumatou and Djabril's health began to improve, and they began to regain their strength. After two months in the hospital, they were released and granted permission to enter the refugee camp.

CHAPTER 9
Life in Kpomasse

"The Kpomasse refugee camp,"
Blema would later recall,
"was like a prison."

WHEN BLEMA AND FATOUMATOU ENTERED THROUGH THE gates of Kpomasse and caught their first glimpse of the makeshift community, their hearts sank. They had been looking forward to the day when they could enter the camp, envisioning a place where they could rest from their sufferings, but from their first glance at the scene before them, it became apparent that their trials were not yet over.

Stepping out of the van, their eyes were drawn to the endless rows of long brick structures that had been constructed by the United Nations to provide housing for the refugees. Hundreds of men, women, and children were wandering around the camp. Each, they knew, had their own tragic story to tell.

A camp official had seen the van drive up and came out to meet them.

"All right, get your things," he ordered. "You'll register at the office and then I'll show you where you'll be staying."

Blema and Fatoumatou obediently followed him to a small stucco building where they filled out several forms and handed them to the official.

"I see you're from Guinea-Bissau," the official noted while looking at the papers.

"Yes," answered Blema.

"We don't see many people from there. You're a long way from home."

"Yes, sir, we are."

"Well, if you'll follow Kwame here, he'll show you to your room. You'll be sharing the room with twelve others, so watch yourselves, follow the rules, and be respectful. We don't want any problems, understand?

"Yes, sir."

"Do you have any questions?"

"My wife and child are hungry," said Blema. "They'll need something to eat."

"Of course. You can pick up rice in the end building when you are settled. There's been a ration on food. Each of you will be given three kilos of rice every month."

"Three kilos!" Blema exclaimed in disbelief. "I don't want to sound ungrateful, but that seems like barely enough to live on!"

"I know it's not much, but there are over five thousand people here in the camp to feed. There are gardens outside in back of the buildings, and we encourage the refugees to grow whatever they can."

The official got up and motioned for them to follow Kwame.

Aware of their concern over the food situation, Kwame led them outside and then offered his own advice.

"Most of the refugees here have plenty to eat," he confided, "but it's not easy; they have to work for it. Many of them are going to the bushes to catch bugs and small field animals to supplement their diet. If you do that, just make sure you don't kill the snakes. If you forage the bushes, you'll find leaves to make soup. I suggest you do whatever you need to do."

Not quite sure if this was given for reassurance or as a warning, Blema and Fatoumatou remained uneasy.

Blema and Fatoumatou followed Kwame toward one of the long buildings. Each building was divided into six rectangular rooms with an entrance door in the front and back of each room. Opening the door to number 28, he ushered them inside.

The room was hot and muggy. As they stepped in, their senses were immediately seized by the smell of dirty, sweaty bodies. Opening their mouths, they sucked in air to avoid taking breaths through their nostrils, lessening the impact of the smell. As they proceeded, they walked past worn mattresses that were lined up against the wall. Individual spaces had been divided by lapas that were hung from wall to wall.

It was mid-afternoon, and many of the residents had come inside to escape the scorching sun. Their eyes glared as Blema and Fatoumatou slowly made their way across the room. Forcing themselves to ignore the unfriendly stares, they continued to follow Kwame until he stopped and pointed down to a single, thin mattress lying on the floor. "This," he told them, "is where you'll be staying." He then leaned in to whisper, "And ignore these people. They'll warm up when you get to know them." Blema and Fatoumatou thanked him, and he turned to leave.

After he had gone, Fatoumatou put Djabril down on the mattress to lighten her load, and she watched him as he snuggled into the blanket that lay on top. Folding the change of clothing that they had brought, she placed it neatly beside the mattress, while Blema went to work hanging a lapa to divide their space from the others. It would be difficult to live in such close quarters, but this would offer them a sense of privacy.

The rest of the day was spent wandering outside as they tried to get a feel for the layout of the camp. When night fell, they made their way back to their little space and settled in.

As others entered the building, the room became filled with the sounds of chattering adults, crying children, and the raised voices from an occasional dispute. Although they felt exhausted, Blema and Fatoumatou knew it would be difficult to sleep.

Because the mattresses had been pushed together to utilize space, Blema and Fatoumatou discovered that if their feet were to wander off the mattress during the night, they would most likely be playing footsies with their neighbor by morning.

Despite the problems of being placed in an overcrowded room, they knew better than to complain. They had seen how others were being forced to live in tents, and they both felt fortunate that they had been assigned to a building. Not only were the tents overcrowded, they provided very little shelter from the elements.

During the rainy season, the tents were a mess. The canvas walls were insufficient in keeping out the rain that poured in, and they became wet, muddy, and cold. When the dry season came, they were hot and filled with dust, mosquitoes, and snakes that wandered in from the bush, so as bad as things seemed to be inside the buildings, Blema and Fatoumatou knew that things could be worse, and they counted their blessings.

For the first few days at the camp, Blema and Fatoumatou worked together to establish a daily routine. This would help make them feel that they had some control over their lives. It would also help them to accomplish as much as they could during the day.

In time, they would grow accustomed to the rhythm of the camp. Blema joined the other men as they worked in the garden and tended to other duties, while Fatoumatou cared for Djabril, cooked, and cleaned. It became her responsibility to fetch the water each day, which was not an easy chore.

Although water had once been available to the refugees through a well that was set up in the camp, it was no longer. Because the single well had served the entire camp population, the overuse of the pump had caused it to wear out, leaving the camp temporarily without water. The Kpomasse refugees were forced to walk to another well that was several miles away.

Fatoumatou dreaded the daily excursions but had no choice in the matter. They needed water, and there was only one way to get it.

In the early mornings, she would strap Djabril to her back, place an empty water vessel on her head and another small one under her arm, and begin the long walk to the well.

From the moment the sun came up, there was a steady stream of women going back and forth to the well, and Fatoumatou could usually find someone to walk with. It was always nice to have company, and the conversation made the miles pass by quickly.

Once the women arrived at the well, they would take turns lowering their containers down inside the pit. When they brought them back up again, the containers were filled with murky black water. Sometimes the water was rust colored or yellow with a disagreeable taste and smell, and Fatoumatou had to force herself to drink it.

It was well known that many people in the camp had been made sick by drinking the tainted water, but like everyone else, Fatoumatou knew she had no choice. When faced with the option of drinking the water or surrendering their lives to thirst, they would drink it anyway.

With her vessels filled with water, Fatoumatou began the more difficult journey home. By now, the sun had risen higher in the sky, and the vessels were made heavy by the weight of the water. When she finally made it back to the camp, she was exhausted. She and Djabril took a much needed rest before it was time to begin preparing their evening meal.

* * * * *

In an attempt to maintain order in the camp, the UN had organized it into communities of nations. They had appointed someone within each community to act as a representative. Many major nationalities were represented, including Congo-Brazzaville, DR Congo, Rwanda, Burundi, Equatorial Guinea, Liberia, Togo, Sierra Leone, Liberia, Sudan, Ogoniland (Nigeria), Guinea, and Chad, as well as twelve minority countries. The twelve minority countries were grouped together and appointed one representative. Guinea-Bissau was considered one of the twelve minority countries.[6]

After Blema and Fatoumatou had been in the camp for three weeks, Blema was approached by the camp chief, who asked if he could meet with him.

"Blema, I understand that you have owned a business and that you ran a pharmacy in Guinea-Bissau."

"Yes, that's right." Blema responded, unsure of where the conversation was leading.

"Well, we're preparing to appoint a representative for the twelve minority countries. We've been asked by the UN to come up with two candidates whom we think could take on this responsibility. The candidates will be involved in an election where one of them would be chosen. We're wondering if you would you be interested in becoming one of them?"

The question had caught Blema off guard. "Well, I don't know. If I were elected, what would be required of me?"

"That's a good question. First of all, you would be responsible to help maintain order within the twelve minority countries' community.

When refugees have concerns about food or medical problems, they would come to you. You would also help resolve conflicts or family issues.

"I see. And what if I were unable to resolve their problems?"

"Well, if it's a small problem, you would turn it over to the protection officer. The more difficult issues are taken to the Minister of the Interior Director or the High Commission Representative. You would also be meeting with representatives from the UNHCR and Benin government officials to apprise them of any concerns that the refugees might have."

"That sounds interesting, but can I ask why you're asking me?"

"Well, to be frank, we're looking for someone with integrity, someone who would be able to work well with the people. We've been watching you since you came to the camp, and from what we've seen, you seem to be able to communicate well with the other refugees. They seem to like you. With your background in business management, we think that you'd be a good fit for this position."

"I feel honored that you'd think so."

"Well, we know that what we're asking of you won't be easy. As you know, this camp is made up of a pretty diverse mix of people. With all of the different languages, tribes, and religions being thrown together, it makes for some complex dynamics. It's going to take just the right person to be able to deal with that."

"Well, can you give me a couple days to think about it?"

"Of course. Just let us know what you decide as soon as you can so we can get someone else if you decide not to participate."

"Fair enough. Thank you."

Blema went immediately to find Fatoumatou to tell her about the meeting.

"Fatoumatou, you won't believe what just happened! I've been asked to be a candidate for the position of Representative of the twelve minority countries."

"Oh, my! That's quite an honor, Blema!"

"Yes, it is," he replied, "and much unexpected."

"What did you tell them?"

"I wanted to talk to you before making any commitments. What do you think?"

"Well, I don't know. It sounds like something that would take up a lot of your time."

"Yes, I'm sure it would."

"What about me and Djabril?"

"I would make time for you, Matou. I know it would be a sacrifice, but when I look around the camp and see all of the people who are struggling, I feel a responsibility to try to make things better; not only for us, but for everyone. This position would give me a chance to try to make a difference."

"You're a good man, Blema. Of course I'll support you."

"Thank you, Matou."

"Who's the other candidate?"

"I'm not sure, but I believe he's a lawyer. There's a good chance that he'll win the election, and then we won't have to worry about it."

"Well, that's certainly one way to look at it."

"But, you know Matou, the more I think about it, I really would like to win. They're placing a lot of trust in me. I just hope that I would be up to the challenge."

"I'm sure you will. God will help you do what needs to be done."

"Thank you, Matou."

Blema accepted the nomination. When the election was held, the ballot count confirmed that Blema had won the vote, and he was thereafter appointed as Representative of the twelve minority countries.

* * * * *

Blema walked into their room in the middle of the day one day to see Fatoumatou laying on the bed with Djabril, crying.

"What's wrong, Fatoumatou?" he asked.

"I've been thinking about the children," she sobbed. "I miss them so much. What are we going to do, Blema?"

"Come here, Matou." Blema put his arm around his wife to comfort her. "I know that it's hard for you to be separated from them," he sympathized. "It's hard for me too."

"It's not fair, Blema! Why did all of this have to happen?"

"I don't know, Matou."

"I just want my children! Why can't we just go back and get them?"

"You know as well as I do that that's not possible. You and Djabril aren't in any condition to try to travel that distance, and for that matter, neither am I. I don't think any of us would survive that journey again."

"But, we need to do something."

"What can we do, Matou? Even if we did get back to Senegal somehow, then what? We couldn't stay there, it's still too dangerous. And you know we can't go back to Guinea-Bissau."

"But I told them we would come back for them, Blema. They're waiting for us. They're going to think that we've abandoned them!"

"It breaks my heart too, Fatoumatou, but there isn't anything we can do about it right now. We need to pray that they'll be safe and hope that someday they'll understand."

"But, what if we never see them again? How can we live with that?" Fatoumatou looked at Blema with pleading eyes. Her face had swollen from crying, and the dark circles that had formed around her eyes made her appear older than her years.

"Let's not think about that. We have to have faith that somehow God will bring us back together."

Fatoumatou wiped her tears with the back of her hand. "I don't see how that's possible."

"Well, frankly, I don't either. But we know that with God, all things are possible. We just have to believe that somehow He will make things work out for us."

Blema pulled Fatoumatou close as she buried her head in his shirt.

"We've seen many miracles. We just have to keep believing that someday we'll have our children with us again. We can't give up hope, Matou. Not now. Our hope is all we have to hold on to."

CHAPTER 10
The Church

"We must not give up hope!" Pastor Bobby admonished his congregation. Blema and Fatoumatou were drawn to this kind and gentle man. They admired him for his unshakable faith and determination to improve living conditions within the camp, and they found great comfort and strength within his messages, taken from the Bible.

These frequent messages of hope always seemed to resonate with them. Since being placed in a seemingly hopeless situation within the camp where they were surrounded by hopeless people, it was sometimes difficult to believe that anything good was ever going to happen in their lives again.

With a gift of natural sanguinity, Pastor Bobby had helped his fellow refugees look at their lives with a different perspective. He made them feel that there was purpose and growth in their sufferings, and at the same time, made them believe that a better life was always just ahead. This mild-tempered, unassuming man was a steady leader and a spiritual giant in the eyes of his congregation, and they all looked to him for guidance.

Pastor Bobby had gathered his little flock shortly after coming to the camp with his family as refugees, and this unlikely band of Christian saints had become like family. Through mutual love and support, they all felt united and had found strength in one another.

In the beginning, the group met in a clearing behind the buildings, but as the congregation grew, there became a need for a larger place to gather. Realizing this need, Pastor Bobby took it upon himself to go to the UN authorities to obtain permission to build and organize a Christian church inside the walls of Kpomasse. With permission granted, he enlisted the help of fellow Christian men and supervised the construction of an open-air, thatch roofed structure, furnishing it with a dozen wooden benches and a wooden pulpit. Not only would this structure provide a place for the worshipers to gather, it would become a refuge in the storms of their uncertain lives.

The congregation gathered often. They met several times during the week to pray together and to teach one another from the scriptures. When someone in the congregation had a special need, all of them would fast and pray for that person. Many had been blessed with healing, emotional strength, and guidance as a result of their fasts and prayers.

When they fasted, the fasts would sometimes last for days. These were performed after the Islamic pattern of fasting, meaning during the daytime they would take no food or drink. They would continue to abstain from these until the sun went down and then partake of a simple meal in the evening. They would neither eat nor drink anything again until evening of the following day.

After Blema and Fatoumatou had been in the camp for nearly six months, they approached Pastor Bobby with a special request of their own. Djabril was not doing well, and they would need the prayers and support of the congregation.

CHAPTER 11
Djabril

DJABRIL'S ALREADY FRAIL BODY HAD BEEN DRAINED FROM THE effects of malaria and malnutrition before he had come to Kpomasse. After several weeks in the camp, insufficient food and the lack of fresh drinking water had caused his health to deteriorate even further, and his condition became critical. Blema and Fatoumatou watched helplessly as their little boy grew more weak and despondent, and they became concerned for his life.

"Blema, we need to do something!" Fatoumatou sat on the bed with Djabril in her arms, nervously jostling him back and forth. Her face was pale with concern.

"I know, Matou. He doesn't look good. We need to get him to a doctor."

"I'm so afraid for him, Blema! Do you think they'll allow us to take him to the hospital?"

"I don't know, but there's only one way to find out."

Wrapping Djabril in a blanket, Blema picked him up and carried him to the UNHCR office. When the officials saw him, they knew that Blema's concerns were justified. Permission was granted to take him back to the hospital in Cotonau.

When Blema, Fatoumatou, and Djabril arrived at the hospital, a blood test revealed what they had feared. Djabril had never fully recovered from the effects of malaria. They were told that he would need a transfusion.

When Blema and Fatoumatou's blood was checked for compatibility, they were relieved to learn that Blema's blood was a match, but when the nurse tried to draw his blood for the transfusion, she was unsuccessful. No matter how much she poked and prodded his arms in search of a productive vein, the syringe repeatedly came up dry. Blema's system had also been taxed by the conditions in the camp.

Because a supply of blood was not available at the hospital, the doctor directed Blema and Fatoumatou to a blood bank in Cotonau where they could purchase the blood and bring it back to the hospital. There was only one problem. The blood was very expensive. It would cost them forty thousand francs, and they had no money.

When Blema and Fatoumatou explained their dilemma to the doctor, he sat them down to clarify the seriousness of the situation. "Djabril is not going to live unless he receives a transfusion," he said bluntly.

When the doctor left, Blema looked over at his son and was suddenly filled with a deep feeling of sadness. He went to him, picked him up, and held him against his chest. Never before had he felt so weak and helpless. Filled with emotion, he gently rocked him back and forth as tears began to flow. "I'm sorry, Djabril," he said softly. "I'm so sorry." With a kiss on his baby's tender cheek, Blema gently placed him back in Fatoumatou's arms, and then turned to leave.

"Where are you going, Blema?" Fatoumatou asked.

"I'm going to town."

"Why? What are you going to do in town?"

"I can't just stand here and watch Djabril suffer like this, Matou. I'm going to go find work and get the money we need for the transfusion. It's his only chance."

After a long day of search, Blema was able to find work at a local restaurant where he was hired to wash dishes. Madam Ade had not planned on hiring anyone, but her heart had been touched by Blema's heart-wrenching situation.

"My baby is sick," he had explained to her. "He will die if he can't get a transfusion. I need to earn forty thousand francs as quickly as possible."

"I'm so sorry," she sympathized. "I wish I could help, but that's a lot of money. I suppose I could make some adjustments and put you to work, but I'm afraid that the most I could pay is ten thousand a month."

"I understand. That's very kind of you, Madam. I'll take the job."

Blema went to work immediately. Leaving Fatoumatou and Djabril at the hospital, he made his way to the restaurant each day, worked his shift, and then returned late at night with food that was left-over from the restaurant. The days passed slowly as Djabril fought to hang on to life.

After a month had gone by, Madam Ade came to Blema to pay him for his work. She smiled as she handed him an envelope. "Blema, you've worked hard. Thank you."

Blema took the envelope and opened it. To his surprise, he found fifty thousand francs inside, well over the agreed amount. He took out the money and looked at Madam Ade. Touched by her kindness, he was suddenly overcome with gratitude. "You'll never know how much this means to me and my family," he managed.

"God be with you, Blema," she said. "You go take care of your baby."

With the money in hand, Blema went immediately to the blood bank to purchase the blood and then went directly to the hospital.

It was late evening by the time he arrived, and the hospital was dark and quiet. As he entered the room, he found Fatoumatou sitting on the bed, holding Djabril in her arms, rocking him back and forth. When she looked up at Blema, her swollen eyes and tear stained face told him that he had come too late.

"Oh, Fatoumatou . . . no!"

He went to her and took Djabril's lifeless body from her arms, and then stood there in disbelief. The small blanket that he was wrapped in was still warm. Blema buried his face in it and wept.

Early the next morning, he called the UNHCR office to make arrangements for transportation back to the camp, but there was no answer. He tried again several times throughout the day, but still, no answer. The office had been closed for a holiday. They would have to find their own transportation.

With Djabril's body still wrapped in the blanket, Blema and Fatoumatou walked out to the street where they saw a man standing beside his parked motorcycle. Blema approached him and asked if he would give them a ride. With money that was left over from the blood purchase, he offered to pay him for his time and gas.

The man looked at them and their bundle suspiciously. "What's wrong with your baby?" he asked. "Is he sick?" Blema knew that if they told him the truth, he would not let them ride.

"He's sleeping," he said.

"All right then, come on."

They mounted the motorcycle and sat pressed against one another on the seat as Fatoumatou held on tightly to Blema with Djabril's lifeless body between them. Awkwardly, they rode to the edge of town where the man stopped and told them he could go no further. Reluctantly, they got off the motorcycle and stood at the side of the road.

Still miles from the camp, Blema hailed a taxi. When a car pulled up beside them, he asked the driver if he would take them to the camp. This driver also wondered about the baby. "He's fine," Blema told him.

Blema pulled out his remaining cash so the taxi driver could see it, and then asked him again.

"All right," the taxi driver said, "get in."

Climbing into the backseat, they settled in for the hour-long drive to the camp. Fatoumatou held her baby's body against her chest and began to shake, overcome by emotion.

"Matou!" Blema warned in a nervous whisper. Reaching down he grabbed her leg, squeezing it firmly. "Shhh!" he said quietly, afraid that the driver might discover their secret and put them out of the car. Fatoumatou choked back her tears and stared straight ahead as they rode the rest of the way in silence.

When they got to the camp, their friends gathered around the taxi to greet them. When they learned that Djabril had died, they were filled with sadness. The women began to wail mournfully and came to Fatoumatou to comfort her. Several men followed Blema as he carried Djabril's body to the back of the building where he would choose a spot to bury their son. The men helped him dig a small grave in the hard soil.

Djabril's small body, wrapped in a blanket, was reverently placed in the grave. Pastor Bobby offered some words of hope and comfort before the last shovel of dirt was placed on the grave. The burial would be followed by seven days of mourning.

The days that followed were difficult for Blema and Fatoumatou.

The loss of their little child weighed heavily upon them, and they were overcome with an unshakable sense of hopelessness. They lost their appetite and had no desire to work around the camp. More than ever they wanted deliverance from the camp. They ached to be near their surviving children and they prayed intently for their welfare.

CHAPTER 12
The Miracle of the Mangos

Hunger plagued the refugees every day, and it never went away. They were hungry when they awoke each morning. They worked and went about their day, hungry. At nighttime, they went to bed hungry. Their daily ration of rice and the few vegetables they received from the garden never did completely satisfy them, and they could only dream of a good meal.

Blema and Fatoumatou had been in the camp for nearly three years and the situation had not improved. In fact, in some respects, it had only grown worse. Benin had experienced a particularly bad growing season the year before, and with an ever increasing population in the camp, food had become unbearably scarce.

"Why doesn't the Lord hear our prayers?" asked Fatoumatou one night as they lay in bed. "Doesn't he know how much we're suffering?" Blema lay by her side wondering how to answer her question, trying to ignore the pangs in his stomach. Without saying a word, he got up and went outside to the bush to pray.

A few days later, he stepped outside of his room to discover a small tree growing near the door. He had not seen it there before. He went closer to examine it and recognized the leaves immediately; he had helped his father plant mango trees when he was a boy. He wondered where the tree had come from. No one had planted it, it just grew.

A few days later, Blema noticed that there were several more trees growing around the camp, and he excitedly announced the news to other refugees. Equally excited about the trees, everyone made sure that they were watered and cared for.

Within a short period of time, the small trees grew and began to put forth a few small mangos. By the next year, the trees were filled with the colorful, sweet fruit. There was no doubt that this had been a gift from God, and the event came to be known throughout the camp as "the miracle of the mangos."

* * * * *

The delicious fruit was a great boon to ward off hunger, but as in all things, too much of a good thing is not good.

During the growing season, the refugees gorged themselves on the mangos and then paid the price for their lack of self-control. Diarrhea ran through the camp like a plague, and with no medication available to them, it became a serious problem.

When the sick refugees came to Blema for help, he became greatly concerned for them. As a pharmacist, he knew that the right medication would cure the problem, but unfortunately, there was no way to obtain it.

Going to the camp authorities as Representative of the twelve minority countries, Blema made a plea for help. The camp authorities expressed their concern and promised to look into the matter, but as the days went by, nothing was done to solve the problem. Finally, Blema decided that he would have to take the matter into his own hands.

One morning, he got up early and boarded a bus that was headed for Cotonau. When he had made his way to the pharmaceutical company, he entering the building and asked to speak with the manager. The woman at the front desk greeted him politely and directed him to a seat where he could wait.

After sitting for some time, the manager finally appeared. As he entered the room, Blema sprang to his feet and crossed the room to where he stood. Offering his hand, he introduced himself and then proceeded to tell him why he had come.

"I'm here on behalf of the refugees at Kpomasse camp," he explained. "Many of our people are sick and dying. They're in desperate need of medication."

"I'm sorry to hear that, Blema. What can we do to help?"

"Well, frankly sir, I was hoping that your company would be willing to donate the medications our people need."

"I see. Well, I can certainly sympathize with your problem, and our company would like to help, but unfortunately, it's not that easy. I'm afraid the matter would have to go through the right channels and be cleared by the UNHCR before we could do anything. We would also have to work through an NGO to do something like that."

"NGO?"

"Nongovernmental Organization."

"I understand. And if I were able to obtain clearance and provide an NGO?"

"Well, then I think that maybe something could be worked out."

"Thank you, sir! Thank you for your time."

Blema returned to the camp and immediately met with the UN High Commission Representative and told him of his meeting with the pharmaceutical company's manager.

"I really believe that they're willing to work with us!" Blema declared.

"Well, how about that! You've done well, Blema. What can we do to help?"

"Well, I've learned that we can't move forward with this until they receive a formal okay from the UNHCR. If you could provide them with the papers they need, that would take care of the first step."

"All right, I'll certainly look into it. What else?"

"From what I understand, an NGO would provide an avenue for the pharmacy to make their donations. With your permission, I'd like to work on getting one set up. My friend, Alphonse, has had some experience with that, and he's expressed an interest in helping me."

"It sounds like you and Alphonse already have that under control."

"Well, I'm sure that we'll have to muddle our way through, but we'll try to figure it out."

"Great. You know, Blema, you're doing a great thing, but we have to realize that getting the pharmaceutical company to donate the medications is only part of the problem. If they actually go through with this, we'll have to appoint someone to be responsible for receiving the medications, and then to see that they're distributed responsibly to the refugees."

"Yes, I've thought of that. I can take care of that."

"I don't know, Blema, that's a huge responsibility, and you're doing so much already."

"Well, to be honest, it's harder for me to stand by and do nothing. These people are suffering, and I know I can help."

"Yes. Well, I guess that it does make sense that you do it. We don't have many pharmacists in the camp."

"Thank you, sir."

"Thank you, Blema. You're doing a great service."

The UN High Commission Representative went to work immediately and provided the pharmaceutical company with the required documents.

Meanwhile, with the help of Alphonse Bamana and Fatoumatou, Blema organized an NGO and they named it "The Feel Better Organization." This would enable the camp to receive donations, not only from the pharmaceutical company, but from various charities, including Catholic Relief and the Red Cross, which would provide food supplies and education on health.

When the pharmaceutical company sent the first donation of medication, Blema felt a great sense of gratitude and satisfaction. He felt that he really was helping to make a difference in the camp.

CHAPTER 13
The Snakes

WE KNOW THAT THE LORD HAS BEEN FAITHFUL TO ANSWER our prayers," Pastor Bobby exclaimed, addressing the congregation, "but He doesn't always answer them in the way we think He should. We have seen His help come in miraculous ways, yet sometimes, rather than taking our problems away, He will choose to bless us with the wisdom and courage we need to solve our own problems."

* * * * *

Each year during the dry season, snakes invaded the camp. Many of the snakes were poisonous, and there had been several reports of deaths that were attributed to snakebite.

Although the problem could have been easily controlled by going through the camp and killing the snakes, the problem was more complex than that.

Within the camp, there was a large population of Voodoos and Jujus. These people regarded the snakes as gods, and to them, killing a snake was considered to be a great offense. There had even been reports throughout the camp of the Jujus killing people and then eating the flesh of those who had committed this horrible transgression. Whether these stories were true or not, the refugees became greatly disturbed, fearful of becoming dinner for the Jujus!

Many of the refugees, not knowing where else to turn, came to the Christians for help. In turn, the Christians sought for the Lord's guidance. As a congregation, they prayed that the He would intervene and take the problem away.

As fervent as was their prayers, the problem did not go away. Not knowing what to do, Pastor Bobby suggested that they gather and hold a fast and prayer vigil, thereby increasing their efforts to gain the Lord's intervention.

The congregation agreed, and they began a fast that very day. It was decided that they would meet at the church at ten o'clock that night. At that time, after praying together, they would separate to continue with their personal prayers throughout the night and then meet once again at five o'clock in the morning to close their prayers.

Blema and Fatoumatou felt a need to participate. That night, they came to the church, fasting, and arrived just before ten o'clock. A prayer was offered, and after listening to a brief message from Pastor Bobby, the congregation separated for their personal prayers.

Fatoumatou went back to her room where she would continue to pray. When Blema had seen that she was safely inside, he went alone to a secluded place in the bush to pray. He found a clearing that was surrounded by thick vegetation and settled in. The place was familiar to him. He had come there so often that it had come to feel sacred to him.

Falling to his knees near a tall baobab tree, Blema raised his head and hands toward the heavens and began to pour his heart out to God. He pled that the Lord would show forth mercy and hear the prayers of his fellow refugees, and that He would drive the snakes from the camp. He expressed his faith that, if it was His will, he knew it could be done.

As he continued to pray into the night, his thoughts eventually turned to his children. Through tears he expressed his pain over their long separation, and he asked the Lord to watch over them and keep them safe. He also prayed for Fatoumatou, asking that she would find comfort and that she would be given the strength to endure her trials. He then prayed for himself, that he would not lose hope.

His prayers continued for several hours until he was overcome by fatigue, and sometime in the middle of the night, he fell asleep.

While lying upon the ground, he began to dream. The dream was vivid and it seemed to go on for a long time. When he awoke, he was able to remember even the smallest detail, and he went immediately to tell Fatoumatou about it.

"Matou," he said, gently shaking her awake. "Matou, listen. I've had a dream."

Fatoumatou sat up to listen.

"I fell asleep in the bush last night and I had a dream. I saw men who were chasing me. They wanted to arrest me so I ran from them. I was so afraid. I ran and ran. I saw a hill and I ran toward it. I began to climb the hill and discovered that it was very steep. As I reached the top, I turned to look at the men and I realized that they were unable to follow me. They couldn't touch me. Eventually they gave up trying and went away.

I then looked down the hill again and saw other men standing down below. One man called to me and said, "Come down, Blema. We will baptize you, and you will be free from sin." As they beckoned to me, I went down to the water and I was baptized.

I then looked up and saw a beautiful building up on a hill. I was told that it was there that I would find the living God. We went inside the building, and one of the men gave me a white shirt. I looked around and saw other men in white shirts. The man told me to trust the Lord, and He would bless me. Then I woke up."

Blema in his white shirt in the Kpomasse camp

"That is an important dream, Blema!"

"Yes, I believe it is. I saw things so clearly! I think the Lord is trying to tell me something. Tomorrow I will go to the village and find a white shirt," he said.

By the next week, the snake problem had not gone away, so the Christians agreed to meet once again, just as they had done the week before.

When they met at the church, Blema was asked to offer the prayer. Feeling a weight of responsibility, he pled with the Lord on behalf of the refugees, asking Him to hear their prayers and relieve them of the snakes. When he had finished, the congregation separated for their own prayers.

Blema went once again to his place in the bush and began to pray. Kneeling upon the ground, he prayed for several hours until he fell asleep, and once again, he began to dream.

In this dream he saw a man who approached him and said, "Blema, you will never leave this camp. You are foolish to believe that you ever will. It is impossible. You will never leave!" Blema awoke with a start was very troubled and distraught by what he had seen.

"It's not true!" he cried out loud. "The Lord will make a way for me!"

His body was trembling and he began to sob as his head and shoulders pulsated to the rhythm of his cries. His tears rolled freely down his face and onto the dry dirt. Lifting his head toward the sky, he cried, "Lord, hear my prayer. Please help me to trust in Thee. I know You can do all things. I know You can deliver me, just as You delivered the people of Israel. Help me, Lord, and deliver me."

Rocking back and forth, he then began to sing:

"Come follow me, praise the Lord,
Come follow me, praise the Lord,
The Lord is good!

"Come follow me, praise the Lord,
Come follow me, praise the Lord,
The Lord is good!"

Blema was filled with emotion as he sang the words to the song over and over again. Each time he repeated the verse, he would begin it by naming one of his children.

"Joseph,
Come follow me, praise the Lord,
Come follow me, praise the Lord,
The Lord is good!

"Mousa,
Come follow me, praise the Lord,
Come follow me, praise the Lord,
The Lord is good!"

A warm feeling washed over him as he continued to sing.

"Oldpa,
Come follow me, praise the Lord,
Come follow me, praise the Lord,
The Lord is good!

"Bangama,
Come follow me, praise the Lord,
Come follow me, praise the Lord,
The Lord is good!"

He continued to sing until he had gone through all of the names of his children. When he was through, he felt calmed by the Spirit. Exhausted from his emotional outpourings, he went back to the house and went to sleep.

Over the next few days, it was evident that the problem with the snakes had still not gone away. For the third time, the Christians agreed to meet to continue with their prayers.

As done previously, they met at the church at ten o'clock in the evening to pray together, and then separated for their own prayers. Blema settled into his place once again and began to pray.

Once again, in the middle of the night, he fell asleep and began to dream. When he had awakened, he ran to the house to tell Fatoumatou about his dream.

"In this dream, I saw a man," he told her. "The man asked, 'What will you do to glorify the Lord when you are resettled in the United

States?' I thought about what I should do and decided I would make a vow to pay tithing, but I was afraid. I had never made a covenant with the Lord before, and I didn't know if it was right, but then I remembered that Jacob had made a vow to pay tithing. Jacob said, 'all that thou shalt give me I will surely give the tenth unto thee'. When I remembered these words, I knew it would be all right, and I made the vow. Then I woke up."

"That is good, Blema. Perhaps I should make a vow to the Lord as well."

"What would be your vow, Fatoumatou?"

"When we are resettled, I vow to fast for two months to show my gratitude and thanks to the Lord."

"That would be a difficult promise to keep, Fatoumatou. Are you sure?"

"Yes, Blema. That will be my vow."

"You are a good woman, Fatoumatou. I know that the Lord will bless us because of your faith."

After the third night of prayers and fasting, the Lord had not rid the camp of the snakes. Instead, he emboldened the Christians to solve the problem on their own. When the sun came up, all of the men gathered their sticks and spears, and went fearlessly about the camp, hunting down and killing the snakes.

When confronted by the Voodoos and Jujus, the Christians told them, "These snakes are not God, and to say so is an offense to God. There is only one God; the God of Abraham!" They then went about boldly killing the snakes in front of them.

The Voodoos and Jujus were so amazed by this courageous demonstration of faith that they stood paralyzed, unable to do anything. Silently, they watched as the Christians cleared the camp of the snakes.

Many of the Voodoos' and Jujus' hearts were softened that day. Afterward, some began coming to church. Young people who had been taught Voodoo and Juju ways from their parents started to question their parents' teachings and became receptive to Christian beliefs. The Christians knew that they had witnessed another miracle.

CHAPTER 14
The Reporter

According to a report that had been put out by the Benin government and given to the United Nations, the Kpomasse Camp was in good order and the people were healthy and well taken care of. When Blema received a copy of the report, he read it in disbelief. The report was inaccurate, and he felt that the camp had been grossly misrepresented. Not all was well in the camp, and Blema wanted the United Nations to know about it.

About that time, a German journalist had also read the report and it had piqued her curiosity. She made arrangements to visit the camp to investigate the claims, planning to come back and write a report of her own.

When the journalist arrived at the camp, Blema was appointed to be the spokesman for the refugees. Escorting her through the camp, he revealed the poor conditions the refugees were living under.

Blema took her first to the water well. It had been repaired, but the water quality was extremely poor and had made the people sick. He then took her to where the food was stored and explained the rations. The amount of food they were given was insufficient, and the refugees were suffering from malnutrition. AIDS had run rampant throughout the camp and had claimed the lives of many adults. The camp was faced with the problem of dealing with the orphans that were left behind.

Pointing out the unmarked graves, Blema talked of the refugees that had died due to malaria and other disease, malnutrition, unfit drinking water, snakebite, and violence.

Deeply affected by what she had seen and heard, the journalist returned to Germany and wrote an article that was published in international newspapers. The article was also picked up by the local Benin newspapers.

Because of this article, the United Nations had a more accurate account of the conditions in the Kpomasse camp. Eventually, some improvements were made.

CHAPTER 15
Deliverance

And the Lord said, I have surely seen the affliction of my people . . .
and have heard their cry . . . for I know their sorrows;
And I am come down to deliver them . . . ,
To bring them up out of that land unto a good land and a large,
unto a land flowing with milk and honey;
Exodus 3:7–8

Of the 2,769 days that Blema and Fatoumatou spent in the Kpomasse refugee camp, not a day had gone by that they had not prayed for deliverance. Deep inside, they believed that the day would eventually come, but after nearly seven years their hope began to wane. Doubt had crept in, leaving them with feelings of discouragement and despair.

They had turned to Pastor Bobby for encouragement, but he had none to give them. He too had become downhearted. Together they decided to fast and pray for strength and to ask specifically for resettlement. Thinking of the others, they decided to invite the whole congregation to join them in a fast and prayer vigil. The congregation agreed to meet at the church every day for prayer and worship.

After several days, the Voodoos and Jujus noticed an increase in activity among the Christians and were upset by it. They threatened them with black magic and told them to stop, but the Christians refused to give in.

The Voodoo and Juju elders then went to the camp official and angrily made the claim that the Christians were causing a disturbance in the camp. A camp official came to Pastor Bobby to investigate the matter.

"I understand that there's a problem between you and the Voodoos and Jujus," he said.

"Yes, sir, I'm afraid there is. But the problem is not with us. We've done nothing to those people."

"Is it true that you've been gathering late at night?"

"Yes, sir."

"Why? What are you doing?"

"We've been praying . . . for resettlement."

"Resettlement? Where in the world did you get that idea? You're not going anywhere. You're causing a disturbance in the camp, and I can't allow it to continue. You need to stop!"

"Respectfully, sir, isn't it our right to worship as we wish?"

"Not when you're disturbing others."

"Well, as much as we want to get along with the Voodoos and Jujus, I don't believe that they should determine how we worship."

"Look, I'm telling you now that if you want to keep your church, you need to stop doing what you are doing."

When the men parted, Pastor Bobby was emotionally drained and upset. He sent the word out to his congregation that they would have to limit their gatherings. They would now only gather on Sunday, but he encouraged them to continue with their daily personal prayers.

The Voodoos and Jujus were not satisfied. They wanted the Christians to stop gathering all together. Because the Christians refused, the conflict continued to grow. The camp official eventually took the matter to the Interior Minister, who then came to Pastor Bobby.

"This has become a real problem," the Interior Minister told him. "For the sake of keeping peace in the camp, you're going to have to discontinue your meetings; at least until things settle down."

"Do you mean all of our meetings?"

"All of them!"

"That isn't right!" Pastor Bobby exclaimed.

"Right or wrong, it doesn't matter. That's the way it's going to have to be. If you don't stop gathering, your church will be shut down for good."

When the congregation heard what had been said, one man suggested that Blema speak to the Interior Minister as Representative of the twelve minority countries. Blema agreed to try.

"It's important that these people be allowed to gather," Blema told the Interior Minister. "They need to be able to pray together. This is what gives them hope. If you take that away from them, what else do they have?"

"I'm afraid we just can't allow it anymore, Blema. It's causing contention in the camp, and it's our responsibility to maintain peace."

"Well, what about the other churches? The Congo and Togo communities have their churches, and there are others. Do they need to stop gathering as well?"

"They're not causing the problem. I've given you my orders, Blema. You'll need to comply!"

"The UN supports our right to worship. If you won't allow us to gather, we'll take the matter up with the UN."

"The UN has made me responsible to maintain order in the camp. If you don't do as I've have asked, your church *will* be shut down."

Discouraged by his threats, Blema went back to Pastor Bobby to tell him what had been said.

"It doesn't look good," Blema said. "I'm not sure what to do."

Pastor Bobby paused.

"You know, Blema, I've been thinking. Do you realize that we're a lot like the Israelites? When the Israelites were being persecuted by the Egyptians, they had to depend on the Lord for their deliverance. And didn't the Lord deliver them?

"Just like Pharaoh, the Interior Minister uses his power to keep us from worshiping God. Pharaoh did everything he could think of to keep the Israelites in bondage, but in the end, he was no match for the Lord's power. And if the Lord is mightier than Pharaoh, isn't He also mightier than the Interior Minister? Or the Voodoos or Jujus, or even the Benin government?

"I know that none of what is happening is making sense right now, but I know that if we put our trust in God as the Israelites did, we too will see our deliverance!"

Blema thought about what Pastor Bobby had said, and he knew that he was right.

One night after Blema and Fatoumatou retired to their bed, Blema went immediately into a deep slumber while Fatoumatou went to her knees to pray. After about an hour, Fatoumatou shook Blema awake.

"Blema, get up!" she said. "You shouldn't be sleeping. You should be praying!"

Blema and Fatoumatou were not the only ones praying. The other Christians in the camp continued to pour out their hearts to God, asking for deliverance. Without the privilege of gathering however, it became difficult for them to remain strong, and some began to lose hope.

Pastor Bobby continued to appeal to the authorities from time to time, asking them to reconsider and reinstate their privileges, but the authorities refused to give in and would not allow them to gather. Eventually, the situation began to wear the Christians down, and in time, many felt defeated.

When the Voodoos and Jujus saw that the Christians were becoming discouraged, they began to revel in their small victory and started taunting them. This only made matters worse for the Christians and added to their discouragement.

The hopeless situation weighed heavily upon Blema, and he became extremely discouraged and depressed. The days seemed to drag on, and with each new day came only more discouragement. After a while, he felt as if he were wading through quicksand and found it difficult to accomplish even the simplest daily chore.

While in the midst of this emotional struggle, he stepped outside one day to see Pastor Bobby running toward him.

"Blema!" he called excitedly. "Did you hear the news?"

"No, I guess I haven't. What news?"

Pastor Bobby paused to catch his breath. "Blema, you won't believe this! This is the day we've been praying for. It's finally happening!"

"What's happening?"

"I've just heard that there are countries accepting refugees! Australia, Canada, Germany, Holland, the United States, and others. The door has been opened for us to resettle. Our prayers are being answered, Blema! We're being delivered!"

As Blema listened, he could hardly believe what he was hearing. Overcome with emotion, he shut his eyes and began to weep. Pastor Bobby went to him and embraced him tightly.

At that moment, the burden of despair that Blema had been carrying was lifted, and he suddenly felt light. Returning the embrace, the men began to laugh emotionally.

"Oh, praise the Lord!" exclaimed Blema. "Our God is a powerful God!"

"Oh, yes!" agreed Pastor Bobby. "Our day has finally come!

CHAPTER 16
The Letter

BLEMA AND FATOUMATOU'S HEARTS RACED AS THEY LISTENED TO the voice over the loud speaker.

"All refugees that are interested in resettling are to come to the office and pick up an application."

Without hesitation, they made their way to the office where a woman handed them each a white slip of paper and a pen.

"When you are finished filling out the form," she told them, "your application will be reviewed by the High Commissioner. He will determine if you are eligible."

Blema and Fatoumatou took the applications to their room and carefully began to fill out the forms. Blema wrote in their names and all the other required information. When he was halfway down the page, he came to a line that read, "List all children and other family members," and he stopped. He read it out loud to Fatoumatou.

"What do we do?" she asked.

This was a dilemma. Over the past seven years in the camp, Blema and Fatoumatou had made numerous attempts to contact their children, but with no success. Without phone service in the camp, it was impossible for them to call. Even if there had been phone service, Kadiatou and Therno had no phone and could not have received their call.

Without mail service in the camp, the only way to send a letter was to make the journey to Cotonau. Blema and Fatoumatou had done this on several occasions, but they had received no response to their letters. They were sure that Kadiatou would have responded if she could have, and they feared that something was wrong. Without communication, their children had become lost to them. They no longer knew where they were, and they had no way to find out.

"Blema," Fatoumatou asked. "Are we doing the right thing?"

"I don't know, Matou. It doesn't feel right to resettle to a different country without our children, but I'm afraid that if we wait to find them, we'll lose our chance to resettle."

Feeling torn, Blema and Fatoumatou decided to consult with Pastor Bobby.

"I can't tell you what to do," he said, "but I believe that the Lord has opened up this opportunity for you. If you don't take it now, you may never leave the camp. Then, how will you ever find your children?"

Blema and Fatoumatou knew he was right. With a prayer in their hearts they filled out the forms, excluding the names of their children, and turned them in.

By February of 2008, Blema and Fatoumatou received word that the High Commissioner had accepted their applications. This would open the door to a seemingly endless series of applications and interviews.

The first interview was conducted by a representative from the Department of Immigration. The interview felt more like an interrogation than an interview. Blema sat nervously as the representative proceeded to ask him questions, and he chose his words carefully before he answered. As he spoke, he felt prompted to know what to say.

While Blema went through his interview, Fatoumatou was having the same experience in another room. The questions made her nervous. She was afraid that if she answered wrongly, she would lose her chance for resettlement. She, too, felt that the Spirit was guiding her words. When one interview was completed, they were scheduled for another.

In the second interview, they stood before the High Commissioner, representatives from the Benin government, and representatives from the Department of Immigration, and the officials took turns asking questions. Blema and Fatoumatou spoke from their hearts and hoped that their statements would be accepted.

A series of interviews referred to as OPE 1, OPE 2, and OPE 3, were then scheduled. During OPE 1, Blema and Fatoumatou's refugee status was confirmed, and the necessary documents were prepared. During OPE 2, they were asked to clarify their refugee status, whether they were political refugees, economic refugees, or if they were in the camp for some other reason. They were also asked about their background, family, schooling, and medical history. Every statement that they made during this meeting was recorded.

Once again, Blema was drilled with questions which were increasingly difficult to answer.

"Why," they asked, "were you attacked by the government soldiers? Were you supporting the rebel troops?"

"No," he replied. "I was a pharmacist in Guinea-Bissau, and I was committed to help anyone who came into the pharmacy. I didn't turn anyone away. There was no way to distinguish a rebel from anyone else, so if I was selling medication to rebels, I didn't know it. I served everyone the same."

For almost an hour, Blema answered question after difficult question.

At the same time, in a separate room, Fatoumatou was being asked questions about the circumstances that had driven her to the camp, her family and relationships, schooling, religion, and so on.

When they went in for their third interview, OPE 3, they were asked to repeat everything they had said during OPE 2. They were told that if the statements that were made in this meeting did not match up exactly to the statements they had made in the previous interview, or that if their spouse's answers did not agree, they would be sent away and the chance to immigrate would be lost.

By the time they finished this series of interviews, they were mentally and physically exhausted, but they were anxious to know if they had successfully passed.

The applicants were instructed to have the heads of the household come to the office the following day to board a motorbus that would take them to the immigration office in Cotonau. There they would receive a letter which would state whether or not they had been approved for immigration.

The next morning, Blema and Fatoumatou awoke early and headed for the office where Blema would board the motorbus. Although Blema had tried to convince Fatoumatou that it wasn't necessary for her to come, she was filled with nervous anxiety, and insisted on seeing him off.

When they arrived at the office, many people had already gathered and were anxious to be on their way. Blema and Fatoumatou made their way to check a list that had been posted on the wall. The list included the names of the all those who were to board the motorbus.

As Blema and Fatoumatou searched for Blema's name, they were astonished to find that it was not listed. Just to make sure, they read through the names over and over again, but to their great disappointment, his name was not to be found. Fearing that for some reason they had already been disqualified, Blema asked the officials why his name was not on the list, but there was no clear answer.

As people began filing onto the bus, Blema moved ahead to join them.

"Blema!" Fatoumatou called after him. "Where are you going?"

"I'm going to Cotonau to get our letter!"

"But your name isn't on the list."

"God doesn't write with a pen, Fatoumatou! He hasn't brought us this far to let us down now."

Just then, one of the officials that stood inside the bus called out to Blema. "What are you waiting for, Blema? You should be on the bus!" Relieved, Blema boarded the bus and took a seat. He sat in tense silence all the way to Cotonau.

Fatoumatou had returned to her room to pray and to wait. Something that her father used to tell her ran over and over through her mind. She could almost hear his voice saying, "Matou, you need to be patient. If you will learn this lesson, you will get along much better in life."

The road to Cotonau seemed to stretch on forever, but when the bus finally arrived, Blema got out, joining the others as they made their way to the immigration office.

The immigration workers were standing outside calling out the names of the candidates as the crowd pressed forward to hear them. One by one, the envelopes were handed out to the refugees.

Blema watched as the envelopes were handed out and was intrigued by the scene. Those who had received letters of acceptance fell into a display of jubilation, laughing, singing, and dancing. Letters of rejection were met with weeping and wailing and mournful cries.

Blema strained to hear his name called, and when he heard it, he moved forward to receive his letter. He took it, grasped it tightly, and held it against his chest. As he did this, the thought came to him, "This envelope contains good news!" He lifted his head and said, "Thank you, Lord!"

When the motorbus returned, several of the candidates had made their way back to the camp before Blema. One of the women candidates saw Fatoumatou waiting outside, and through tears she told her that she had been to Cotonau. "My application has been denied," she cried, "Yours has also been denied!"

Assuming that the woman had spoken to Blema, Fatoumatou's heart sank. She sat down on the ground and was about ready to give into tears when she looked up and saw Blema running toward her. He was holding the letter up, waving it through the air.

"Fatoumatou," he called out excitedly. "We're going! We're going to the United States!"

Fatoumatou looked at the unopened envelope and then to him in confusion.

"How do you know that, Blema? You haven't opened the letter!"

"I don't need to open the letter. I know we're going!"

Fatoumatou stared at him in disbelief, afraid that he had lost his mind.

"Open the letter, Blema!"

"Where's your faith, Fatoumatou? Don't you believe that we are going to the United States?"

"Yes, I believe it, but I'd like to see the letter!"

"We should give thanks, Fatoumatou. Our God is truly powerful!"

"Blema! Please open the letter! PLEASE!"

Blema stepped back, took the envelope and tore off the end.

"Well," he said, "It says here," a broad smile came over his face, "that we have been accepted! We're going to the United States!"

CHAPTER 17
Leaving Kpomasse

A slightly overweight, fair-skinned man stood on a box and prepared to speak to the small group of refugees who had gathered in the camp.

"Congratulations!" he began enthusiastically. "You have been chosen to come to the United States."

The man had come as a representative of the United States government and was in charge of immigration. He had been assigned to orientate the qualified refugees and prepare them for immigration.

"You will be going to the land of freedom, the land of democracy," he continued. "It is the land of milk and honey. It is also a land of opportunity, but it will be up to you to make the most of it."

Blema tried to concentrate on what was being said, but on an empty stomach, he heard nothing after "milk and honey."

There were still papers and forms to fill out and medical examinations to go through before they could leave the camp. They would be medicated for malaria and given an antibiotic before they would be allowed to travel. They had not been told specifically where they would be going, and they would not find out until they arrived at the airport and received their plane tickets.

When the day finally came, it was a day of rejoicing, and the excitement could be felt among the refugees. Friends in the camp had gathered around Blema and Fatoumatou to say good-bye and wish them well. One of Blema's good friends came to him and embraced him.

"I'm so happy for you, Blema." He said sincerely. "You know, this reminds me of Joseph of old."

"Oh?" Blema asked, confused. "How's that?"

"Well, can you remember how he was cast into prison along with the chief butler and the chief baker?

"Yes."

"When the butler and baker had dreams they couldn't understand, they asked Joseph to interpret them. Joseph told the baker that he would be put to death, but he reassured the butler that he would be set free. Just before the butler left the prison, Joseph told him, 'Think on me when it shall be well with thee.' So it is with you, Blema . . . remember us."

A sudden pain filled Blema's heart. He would miss these people whom he had come to love so dearly. It was difficult to leave when he knew that many of his friends would have to remain in the camp with no prospects for a better life.

"I will, brother," he said as they embraced.

Blema and Fatoumatou had prepared themselves the best they could for travel. They had put all of their papers in order, packed their few belongings, and dressed in their very best clothing. They were shuttled by bus to the airport, and when they arrived, they were surprised to see that a large group of people had gathered and were waiting for them. News of the immigrations had spread quickly throughout Benin and many people from Cotonau and surrounding towns and villages had come to witness the momentous event.

Blema and Fatoumatou walked through the crowds, following an escort into the airport where they would pick up their tickets. Once inside, they stood and waited until someone called Blema's name and handed him their tickets.

"Where are we going, Blema?" Fatoumatou asked anxiously.

Blema turned the tickets over until he saw the name of the city.

"We're going to Boise, Idaho, " he replied, smiling.

For the past few days, there had been much speculation among the refugees about where in the United States they would be going. They had heard talk of immigrants being sent to California, Arizona, Illinois, and Texas, but no one seemed to know where Boise, Idaho, was.

"Blema, why would they send us to a place that no one has heard of? Are they going to send us to the bush?"

"I don't know, Fatoumatou. We'll have to find a map."

A map was being passed around among the refugees, and after some search, Blema was able to locate Boise.

"Here it is, Fatoumatou," he said while pointing at the map. "It's close to Washington. I think we're going to be living by the president!"

Just then, they heard a familiar voice calling out their names. They looked up to see their friends that they had not seen for many years approaching them. Their friends had been living in Cotonau and had come to see the travelers off. They were surprised to see Blema and Fatoumatou standing among the travelers with their tickets in hand.

"Blema, Fatoumatou, what are you doing here?" asked Dernard.

"We're going to the United States," Blema replied, still not believing it himself.

"Are you kidding? Really? That's wonderful, Blema! Where are you going?"

"We're going to Boise, Idaho."

"Aaaah! . . . . . Where's that?"

Blema placed his finger on the map.

"Blema, I think you're going to the bush!"

Fatoumatou was excited to see Akeelah, and the friends embraced.

"I'm so happy for you, Fatoumatou!" Akeelah said. "Have you talked with your children?"

"No, Akeelah. I haven't heard from my children since I left Senegal years ago. We believe they're still with my sister, but and we haven't been able to contact them. To be honest, we don't know where they are."

"Your children aren't in Senegal, Fatoumatou. I was talking with your brother, Kilarou, and he told me that your children were living with Mamadou and his family in Labe."

"Labe? Why would they be in Labe?"

"Apparently, there were big problems in Senegal, and from what I understand, Kadiatou and Therno were forced to leave their home. They sent the children to live with your brother, Mamadou. I know Mamadou has a phone, but I don't have his number. I do have Kilarou's number, though, and I know that he would have it. Would you like Kilarou's number?"

Fatoumatou stood in silent disbelief, trying to absorb what she was hearing. Suddenly she began to cry.

"Matou," Blema asked, "what's the matter?"

"Mamadou has the children, Blema."

"What? Why would they be with Mamadou?"

"I don't know, but we can get his number from Kilarou. We'll be able to call them!"

"Oh, praise the Lord! We will, Fatoumatou. As soon as we are settled, we will!"

Blema and Fatoumatou bid an affectionate farewell to their friends and made their way through security and found their seats inside the plane. They buckled themselves in their seats and waited anxiously for the plane to take off.

When the plane began to move, Blema and Fatoumatou grasped the armrests and held on tightly as the plane shuttled down the runway and left the ground, climbing rapidly into the hazy African sky. Once they were in the air, they relaxed but looked constantly out the window, amazed by the scene below. Throughout their flight, they talked about their children and wondered what they would say when they spoke to them again.

When they arrived in Paris to change planes, representatives from the International Organization of Migration (IOM) were there to meet them. They made sure that the transfer went smoothly and that Blema and Fatoumatou were safely on the plane that would take them to Chicago, Illinois, where they would stop for a short layover.

As they boarded the international plane in Paris, they were astounded by its size. Walking down the seemingly endless aisle, they took their seats at the back of the plane. A friendly flight attendant walked by, welcoming them and making sure they were comfortable.

When the plane had ascended, the flight attendant came by once again to offer them a meal. Blema and Fatoumatou took the plastic containers from her and placed them on the small adjustable tables that were affixed to the back of the seats in front of them.

When they opened the lids of their meals, they were struck by the aroma from the warmed chicken and gravy, mashed potatoes, vegetables, rolls, and butter. Blema and Fatoumatou looked at the food and then at each other. It all seemed surreal. Fatoumatou began to laugh with emotion as tears came to her eyes. Soon, Blema joined her, and the two laughed and cried over their bounteous meal. How they had dreamed of this day. After a prayer of thanks, they quickly devoured the food. It was delicious.

When they had finished, the flight attendant came by once again to collect their trays and was surprised to see that they had been cleaned from every trace of food. She asked if they would like another meal. Blema and Fatoumatou grinned and gratefully accepted her generous offer.

The second round of food was as delicious as the first. This time they ate slowly, savoring every bite. For the first time in many years, their bellies were uncomfortably full.

When Blema and Fatoumatou arrived in Chicago, there were representatives from the IOM waiting for them, just as there had been in Paris. They thanked them for their help as they boarded the flight that would take them to their final destination.

Blema had gotten a seat by the window, and was delighted to watch the varied topographical scenes pass by below. Fatoumatou was content to rest. It was night when the plane began its final descent into Boise. Blema woke Fatoumatou up and pointed out the window. "We're landing," he said excitedly. Fatoumatou stretched her neck to get a better view.

"What do you see, Blema?" she asked, impatiently. "Are we landing in the bush, or in a village?"

"I don't know. There are a lot of lights. It looks like a city."

As they came closer, they could see a grouping of tall buildings at the base of the mountains.

"We *are* in a city, Fatoumatou!" Blema exclaimed. "And it's very nice!"

When Fatoumatou could see the view, she was seized by emotion and fell silent until they landed. Tears trickled down her cheeks.

"We're home, Blema!" Fatoumatou exclaimed. "We've finally come home!"

* * * * *

The International Refugee Committee (IRC) had made arrangements to have their representatives receive Blema and Fatoumatou at the Boise airport and take them to an apartment that had been prepared for them. The apartment was located off of Vista Avenue, just a few miles from the airport.

The representatives, a man and his wife, greeted Blema and Fatoumatou warmly, and ushered them to a waiting van. Within minutes, they arrived at the apartment. When Blema and Fatoumatou walked through the door, they were amazed by what they saw.

"Oh, my!" Fatoumatou exclaimed, "We will be living better than the president!"

The apartment had been scantily furnished with used furniture, a few kitchen and eating utensils, personal hygiene items, and some cleaning supplies. The refrigerator had been stocked with food. When the woman representative opened the refrigerator door, they were surprised and delighted to see that it was filled with roasted chicken, cheese, milk, and various fruits and vegetables.

Blema and Fatoumatou were then led through the apartment and instructed on how to use the shower, turn on the stove, and set the thermostat. When the representatives were ready to leave, Blema and Fatoumatou thanked them over and over again for their help. Shutting and locking the door behind them, they scurried to the refrigerator to enjoy their first meal in their new apartment.

CHAPTER 18
Resettled

From the minute they stepped onto American soil, Blema and Fatoumatou marveled over the miracle that had brought them to their new home. They felt a deep sense of gratitude and of optimism as they considered the prospects of building their lives anew . . . but not always. Their joy was tempered by an underlying sense of loss and sadness over leaving their homeland and the people they knew, knowing deep down that they might never return. They were especially saddened at times by the realization that they were an ocean away from their children, and they wondered again if they had done the right thing. When heartache and fear from the unknown future fell upon them, they fought these feelings with the courage and faith that had been won through the trials of their past. Their challenge was to look forward and not back.

Over the course of the first few weeks, they worked closely with the IRC, who helped them to adjust to their new way of life. The IRC had committed to help support them financially and offered life training for the first eight months of their resettlement. English classes were also made available to them, and they were taught how to get around town by using the bus system. Bryson, an employee of the IRC, took them to the post office and showed them where they could buy stamps and send letters. He took them to shop for groceries and instructed them on how to use the debit card that had been issued to them by the IRC to make purchases.

Determined to take advantage of every opportunity open to them, they quickly signed up for English classes. Blema had learned some English while in Africa, but his vocabulary was limited, and he didn't feel comfortable using what he knew. Fatoumatou knew no English at all.

After Blema and Fatoumatou had attended several English classes, Bryson was surprised to find how well Blema was speaking. Because the financial support being given by the IRC was temporary and would only last for eight months, Bryson suggested that perhaps he should forgo the classes and look for a job. Although Blema still felt awkward using the new language, he also felt that the eight months of assistance would fly by quickly, and agreed that this would be a wise move.

To help Blema with his job search, Bryson took him to the Department of Labor and introduced him to Lana, one of the employees there. Lana taught job search skills to the refugees and had been instrumental in helping them find employment. Bryson helped Blema sign up for her class.

At the end of one of her classes, Lana informed the job seekers that Wal-Mart was hiring. She offered to help anyone who was interested in the job to fill out an application, and Blema was one of the first to take her up on it.

"I think you might have a good chance of being hired," she told Blema, encouragingly.

Since Blema didn't have a phone, he had put Bryson's phone number on his application as a contact number. A few days after the application was submitted, a Wal-Mart employee called Bryson with a message. They were calling to request an interview with Blema.

Bryson quickly relayed the message to Blema, who was very pleased by the news. He promptly returned the call, and an interview was set for October 17th at 1:00 p.m.

For days, Blema fretted about the upcoming interview. Still feeling tentative about his ability to speak English, he was afraid that he wouldn't be able to communicate well enough to answer the questions he would be asked. He began studying English during every spare moment, desperately trying to enlarge his vocabulary.

"Fatoumatou, I'm worried." Blema confided. "I don't know if I can do this."

"You'll do all right, Blema," Fatoumatou reassured. "I'm praying for you."

On the day of the interview, Blema dressed in his best clothes and met with Lana, who had graciously agreed to take him to Wal-Mart.

When Blema and Lana arrived, they went inside the store and proceeded directly to the office. The manager stood up when he saw them standing at the doorway.

"You must be Blema Fangamou?" The manager greeted as he extended his hand.

Blema took his hand and shook it firmly. "Yes, sir. Hello."

The manager motioned for him to take a seat across the desk from his. Lana quietly took a seat in the corner of the room to keep from being a distraction.

"Well, Blema," the manager began. "Tell me about yourself. Where are you from?"

"I'm from Guinea-Bissau, West Africa," he said. Blema then spoke briefly about his recent resettlement to Boise, while the manager listened with interest. When he had finished, the manager proceeded to ask him questions about his skills, previous work experience, and about his work ethic.

Blema's English flowed as he answered the questions. When the interview was over, he felt confident that he had done well. The manager smiled and thanked him for coming in.

"We'll let you know of our decision," he said.

As Blema and Lana walked out of the building, Lana turned to Blema and exclaimed, "Blema, that was amazing! I didn't know that you had such a large vocabulary."

"I don't!" Blema responded. "Those words were given to me, Lana."

Several days went by before Bryson received another call from Wal-Mart to schedule Blema for a second interview. Again, Lana took him, and the second interview seemed to go as well as the first.

"Well, Blema," the hiring manager said as he stood to shake his hand at the conclusion of the interview. "I think that you would be a great asset to Wal-Mart. Welcome aboard."

Blema was elated to learn that he had been hired. He was told that he would start out by working in the coolers at night. It would be a difficult job, but it would provide a steady income, and he was pleased to have it.

Now, with money coming in, Blema and Fatoumatou started making plans. They decided that, if they were careful with their money and saved all that they could after paying bills, it wouldn't take long for them to afford something that they had only dreamed of for weeks. After two months of saving, they were able to purchase a phone, sign up for phone service, and obtain a phone card that would allow them to call Africa. They could hardly wait to call their children!

CHAPTER 19
Reconnected

"Hello, who is this?"

"This is Sekouna."

"Sekouna! This is your father, Blema Fangamou!" Blema could barely contain his emotion as he spoke.

"What?"

"I'm your father. I'm calling you from the United States."

"This can't be my father. My father is dead."

"No, Sekouna. It's me. I'm here with your mother."

"How can that be? My father died years ago. There were witnesses at his burial."

"That's not true. Your mother and I were in a refugee camp in Benin for many years. We've been resettled now in the United States."

After a long pause, Blema could hear Sekouna call out to his brother.

"Kamonan, come here quickly. This man says he is our father!"

"What?" Kamonan reached over and took the phone from Sekouna. "Hello, who's this?"

"Hello, Kamonan. This is your father, Blema Fangamou. How are you?"

"Father? Is this really you?"

"Yes, it is."

"We thought you were dead!"

"I know, I'm sorry. Your mother and I are very much alive. We're in the United States. How are you, son? Are you well?"

"Yes, I'm well."

"And your brothers and sister?"

"Yes, everyone is doing well."

"Good. I'm here with your mother and she's very anxious to speak to you. Say hello to your mother." Blema handed the phone to Fatoumatou.

"Hello?" Fatoumatou said nervously.

"Mother?"

Fatoumatou was shaken by the sound of Kamonan's voice. It had become deep, unlike the child's voice that she had remembered from so many years ago.

"Mother, I can't believe it's you!" Kamonan cried.

"Oh, Kamonan. I can't tell you how I've missed you! It's so good to hear your voice. How are you, son?"

"I'm doing well."

"Oh, I'm so happy to hear it. Where are the others? Are they there?"

"No, they're not here right now."

"Oh!" Fatoumatou felt deflated.

Hearing the disappointment in his mother's voice, Kamonan quickly added "But, if you'll call back tomorrow, I'll make sure that they're here. We'll all wait for your call."

"That would be wonderful!" Fatoumatou exclaimed.

The phone was passed back and forth from Kamonan to Sekouna on one end and of the line, and from Blema to Fatoumatou on the other. The conversation continued until the phone card ran out, bringing the call to an abrupt end.

The next day, Blema bought another phone card, and he and Fatoumatou made the second call. Sekouna again answered the phone.

"Hello, Father!" he said, excited to hear his father's voice once again.

"Hello, Sekouna. How are you today?"

"I'm doing good. Everyone is here now. We told them about your call, and they're anxious to talk to you."

Sekouna passed the phone to his brother.

"Hello, Father?" said Joseph.

Blema didn't recognize the unfamiliar voice on the line.

"Hello! Who is this?" he asked.

"This is Joseph."

Blema and Fatoumatou were filled with joy as one by one they spoke to Joseph, Oldpa, and Mousa for the first time in over ten years. Then it was Bangama's turn to speak to her parents. She spoke to first to Blema.

"Hello. . . Father?"

"Yes. Hello, Bangama." There was no answer. Blema could only hear Bangama's muffled cry through the receiver.

"Bangama, are you there?" he asked.

"Yes," she sobbed. "Where is my mother?"

"She's here. Would you like to speak to her?"

"Yes."

Fatoumatou took the phone, anxious to speak to her daughter.

"Hello, Bangama," she said.

"Mother, where are you?"

"We're in the United States."

"Why did you leave us? Bangama asked angrily. "You said you would come back for us, but you didn't. You left us alone. You abandoned us!"

Unable to answer, Fatoumatou handed the phone to Blema.

"No, Bangama," answered Blema. "We did not abandon you. We wanted to come back for you, but we couldn't."

"If you wanted to come for us, why didn't you?"

"You were much too young to understand what happened. Someday we'll try to explain it to you. I'm sorry for what you've been through, but the Lord knows, we did not abandon you."

"Will you come for us now?" she asked.

"I wish we could. There isn't anything in this world that we'd like more, but I'm afraid that might not be possible. I can only give you my word that I will do everything I can to try to make that happen someday, but I'm afraid that I can't make any promises."

Blema's comments were met with silence.

"We love you, Bangama. We love all of you. We'll talk often, and I'll send money whenever I can."

The calls to Africa became a daily event, or at least as often as Blema could afford to buy the phone cards. The calls helped fill a place in Blema and Fatoumatou's hearts that had been empty for a very long time.

CHAPTER 20
Fellow Christians

Blema and Fatoumatou seemed to be adapting well to their new home in the United States. They felt grateful for the changes that had taken place in their lives, and yet, they were finding that even in the land of opportunity, things weren't always easy. With Blema's income from Wal-Mart and the financial aid they had been receiving from IRC, they had managed to keep their heads above water, but just barely. When the IRC benefits ran out several months later, they felt like they were sinking.

Fatoumatou knew that Blema was worried. Not knowing what else to do, she told him that she wanted to go to work. After much thought, finally he agreed. Not only would the extra income help their financial situation, but the experience would allow Fatoumatou an opportunity to be around people who could help her learn English.

Blema had heard about an employment center located on the other side of town, and he suggested that Fatoumatou go there. Following his instructions, she boarded the city bus the following day and made her way to the LDS Employment Resource Center.

* * * * *

It was March of 2009, and the economy in Boise had just taken a down-turn. Since many people in the valley had lost their jobs in consequence, the LDS Employment Resource Center had become a hub of activity, and there seemed to be an endless stream of people coming in and out of the doors each day.

Brother and Sister Pauline, missionaries at the center, looked up one day to see a tall, dark, and poised woman enter the heavy glass entrance door. She stood at the doorway, dressed in a colorful, mid-length skirt and blouse. Her hair was neatly braided, and she looked as if she had just stepped out of a page of a National Geographic magazine.

Brother Pauline walked over to greet her while Sister Pauline continued her work behind the counter.

"Hello," he said pleasantly. "Welcome."

In a low voice, dripping with a rich African accent, Fatoumatou responded with, "Aallooo."

"What can I do for you?" he asked.

Fatoumatou just smiled.

"Do you speak English?"

When she didn't respond, Brother Pauline suspected that "hello" the only English word in her vocabulary.

"*Bonjour*," she finally said timidly, not knowing what else to say.

"Ahhh, you speak French!"

"*Oui*."

"*Comment-allez vous aujourd'hui?*"

Fatoumatou's face lit up.

Brother Pauline had taken French classes in high school, but that was forty-five years ago, and he scrambled pull it back into his memory.

"Are you looking for work?" he asked in slow, broken French.

"*Oui*."

"*D'accord*. Let's see what we can do." Brother Pauline pulled out an intake form that required her basic information, and he asked if she could fill it out. When he handed it to Fatoumatou, she just looked at it with a blank stare, unable to read or write. As much as Brother Pauline wanted to help her, he knew that without basic English skills, she would not have a chance at even the lowest level jobs.

Doing the best he could to help her fill out the form, Brother Pauline placed it carefully in the file and then offered her a few words of encouragement. He then bid her "good day." Unfortunately, he didn't know what else he could do for her.

Several days later, he was surprised to see her appear once again, but this time she wasn't alone. She had come with Blema.

Brother Pauline walked across the room and met them at the door. "Fatoumatou, you've come back!" he said.

"*Oui.*"

"And who is this?"

Blema offered his hand, and with a thick, French-African accent, said, "I am Blema Fangamou."

Blema was dressed in a suit and tie which was clean but well used. The coat was the color of dark chocolate, almost matching the color of his skin. Although the suit was slightly too large, it seemed to complement his small, solid frame.

"Hello, Blema." Brother Pauline greeted. "It's nice to meet you. What can I do to help you?"

"I'm looking for work." he said, matter-of-factly. "My wife also needs work."

"I see. Well, why don't you both come and have a seat, and we'll see what we can do."

Leading them to a small round table, Brother Pauline offered them a chair and then sat and listened attentively as Blema explained his situation. Things had become difficult, he explained. Although he was working at Wal-Mart, the job was not full time, and he needed to find a second job.

Brother Pauline waited until he had finished and then made some suggestions of where he might begin his job search. He reassured him that he would help them as much as it was within his ability to do so.

Leading them on a tour of the employment center, he pointed out the resources that were available to them there. He then directed them to a computer where he helped them search the job listings for potential job leads.

Blema and Fatoumatou were there for over an hour. As they prepared to leave, they gathered up the information Brother Pauline had given them and expressed their appreciation for the time he had taken with them.

"It's been my pleasure." Brother Pauline replied. "I'll keep my eyes open for anything that might come up."

Sister Pauline smiled as she listened to her husband speak with Blema. She was delighted to hear them communicate with each other, both speaking in broken languages. There was no way that she could have foreseen that these two men, a French-speaking Mandinka from Africa, and a gray-haired Mormon who had been born and raised in West Virginia, would soon become friends, and in many respects, as close as brothers.

* * * * *

Over the next few weeks, Brother Pauline called Blema occasionally to inform him of job leads, but unfortunately, the job opportunities had become few and far between.

In the meantime, Blema and Fatoumatou had reconnected with some friends that lived nearby. Kakou and Kafui DeSousa had also been refugees in the Kpomasse camp, and although Blema and Fatoumatou had known them for years, they had not been close friends in Africa. Now that they had resettled however, they came to lean on each other in their new environment.

Kakou and Kafui had recently started a small business importing hand woven baskets, clothing, and jewelry from Africa to resell in Idaho. Blema and Fatoumatou were inspired by their business undertaking, and wanted to do the same. They ordered colorful handmade sandals from the same region in Africa, and the two couples made plans to attend an upcoming event where they could sell their merchandise.

Brother and Sister Pauline had met Kakou and Kafui at the employment center, and had encouraged their entrepreneurial ventures. When the Paulines heard about their plans to attend the show, they offered to take them to the event since none of them could drive.

The morning of the festival was beautiful and clear. Brother and Sister Pauline drove to Kakou and Kafui's apartment just before the sun came up and helped them load their merchandise into their gray Chevy Equinox. When they went to pick up Fatoumatou, she was ready and waiting by the door. Because Blema was working that day, she would be attending the event without him.

With the car loaded to the roof, the five of them squeezed into the seats and headed for the Center on the Grove.

The annual World Refugee Day festival in Boise was a grand event, and one that the refugees looked forward to and worked hard for all year. For weeks before the festival, refugees from Sudan, Congo, Somalia, and regions of West Africa, practiced and perfected their dancing, traditional music, poetry, and storytelling performances. These were to be presented on temporary stages that were set up in the center of the grounds. Refugees from all over would man the dozens of booths that had been set up along the walkways, allowing them to showcase a fascinating variety of crafts, clothing, jewelry, and ethnic cuisine from their various countries.

Kakou, Kafui, and Fatoumatou had set a booth alongside the others. They were proud to take part in the event by displaying and selling the merchandise that represented the Congo and West Africa.

They had barely gotten their booth set up and in order when people started to show up. A few trickled in at first, but before long, hundreds filled the grounds, and it became lively with activity.

Fatoumatou at the World Refugee Day Celebration in Boise. Used by permission.

Many curious people walked past Kakou, Kafui, and Fatoumatou's booth. Some stopped, anxious to speak with them about their country and culture. Kakou, Kafui and Fatoumatou often encouraged the event goers to put on their clothing and jewelry, and then posed with them for pictures. They were delighted when someone actually bought their merchandise.

When the event was over, Kakou and Kafui had sold many of their things, but sadly, Fatoumatou, had sold only two pairs of sandals.

The Paulines drove them back home, stopping first at Kakou and Kafui's apartment where they helped unload the boxes while congratulating them on their success.

When they arrived at Fatoumatou's apartment, Blema was there and met them at the door. "Please, come in," he said as he took a box from Sister Pauline and then led them inside.

The apartment was small, simple, and well kept. The front room was furnished with a floral patterned couch on one side and a small rose-colored loveseat on the other. A ten inch black and white television set sat on a short corner table. The walls were bare, except for one picture that hung on the main wall. It was a picture of a violin along with the poem, *The Touch of the Master's Hand.* The room was extremely warm, and a small box fan ran steadily to move the sultry air.

Fatoumatou made her way quickly to the middle of the room and encouraged her guests to sit.

"*Merci beaucoup*, Fatoumatou," said the Paulines as they took a seat on the rose-colored loveseat. Fatoumatou sat with Blema on the floral couch.

"We've really enjoyed spending the day with Fatoumatou," Brother Pauline told Blema. "It's too bad you weren't able to come."

"Yes," Blema replied, "I would have liked to, but I can't miss work."

"Yes, we understand. We feel bad that more of your things didn't sell today. We know that you were depending on making those sales."

"Yes, that's true."

"Are you two going to be all right?" Sister Pauline asked with concern.

"Oh, yes." Blema answered. "The Lord will take care of us."

"Blema, I know this off the subject," interjected Brother Pauline, "but do you mind if I ask . . . are you Christian?"

"Yes, we are."

"Ahh, very good. I guess that's something we have in common."

A broad smile came over Blema's face. "That's good!" he exclaimed. He turned to Fatoumatou and told her what Brother Pauline had said in French, and she smiled.

"You know, Blema," Brother Pauline continued, "we really don't know much about you. You've told us that you're here as political refugees. Where in Africa did you come from?"

"We've come from Guinea-Bissau. Things are not good there." Blema looked away with a pained expression.

"We're sorry to hear that." Sister Pauline sympathized.

"Yes," agreed Brother Pauline, "but were glad that you're here now,"

"Thank you."

"We'd like to help you in any way we can. Would you let us know if there is anything else we can do?"

"Yes, I will. Thank you," Blema said. "You've both been very kind."

CHAPTER 21
A Most Important Book

* * * * *

THE LDS EMPLOYMENT RESOURCE CENTER IS LOCATED IN THE same building as Deseret Industries. Whenever Brother and Sister Pauline were scheduled to work there, it was one of the highlights of Brother Pauline's day to wander over to the D.I. during a break to see if he could find something new at "Tiffanys."

One day, during one of his treasure hunts, he strolled over by the book shelves and spotted a Book of Mormon in French. Because it was not every day that a French edition of the Book of Mormon showed up, he was surprised to see it there. The minute he saw it, he thought he knew exactly who it was intended for, and he immediately purchased the book.

"Are there ever times in your life when you feel that God has placed you in a certain place, at a specific time, to do something important?" Brother Pauline asked his wife one day.

She looked at him and smiled. "Yes, I think I do." It warmed her heart to see her husband's face glow as he spoke. She thought she understood just what he meant. As often as they had prayed to become instruments in God's hands, it was wonderful to realize that sometimes they were.

The next day, with the Book of Mormon in hand, the Paulines went to visit the Fangamous. When they knocked on the door, Fatoumatou answered. Her face lit up when she saw their familiar faces.

"Aalloo," she said, "Hoow are yooou tewdaay?"

"Fatoumatou! You're speaking English!" Brother Pauline exclaimed. "That's very good!"

Fatoumatou beamed and laughed with delight, obviously pleased with herself.

When Blema heard talking at the door, he came in to join them. He then motioned for them to take a seat.

"How are you, Blema?" Brother Pauline asked.

"I'm doing good, thank you."

"We were thinking about you and Fatoumatou today and thought we would come by."

"I'm happy you did. You're always welcome."

"Blema, I've been thinking about our conversation the other day. You told us that you are Christian."

"Yes."

"Well, we were wondering . . . are you and Fatoumatou attending a church?"

"Yes. We go with our friends."

"Wonderful. I know there are a lot of good churches in our community. I'm glad that you've found one."

"Yes, we like it there."

"Good."

"Where do you go?" Blema asked.

"Well, Christi and I are members of the Church of Jesus Christ of Latter-day-Saints. Have you ever heard of it?"

"No, I don't believe so."

"Well, Blema, to be honest, one of the reasons we came here today is to share a book with you and Fatoumatou, one that is very important to us. We certainly don't want to impose it upon you, so we'll only share it with you if you're interested."

"I see. May I see it?"

"Yes, certainly." Brother Pauline handed the Book of Mormon to Blema. Blema took it and studied the cover. "What is it about?" he asked.

"It's about Jesus Christ. It's a record of many ancient people who knew about Him and believed in Him, even before He was born. I know that you believe in the Bible. I've heard you quote from it."

"Is it like the Bible?"

"Yes, in many ways it is. The Bible is a witness of Christ. The Book of Mormon is another witness of Christ. Both contain the words of God."

"Oh?"

"I've also brought you a pamphlet to help explain where this book came from. It's about Joseph Smith, the man who translated the ancient records. It's because of him that we're able to have these writings now."

"Aahh, that's very interesting. Yes, I would like to read it."

"Well, before we give it to you, I want to make sure that you know that we consider you our friends, and that our friendship isn't based on whether you accept this book or not."

"Yes, I understand."

"Good. Well, I hope that you'll take time to read it. It truly is a powerful book. We'd like Fatoumatou to read it as well, but we know that she can't read. Would you mind sharing it with her?"

"No, I would be happy to."

"Blema, I know that God has answered your prayers in the past. When you read this book and pray about it, He'll let you know if it is truly from Him."

"Yes, I believe that's true," said Blema. "I will read it. Thank you."

CHAPTER 22
The Accident

Boise is a beautiful place in the springtime. When the snow melts off the mountains and the spring rains come, the surrounding hills turn a soft, pale green. When set against a blue sky, it creates a pleasant backdrop for the city. Down in the valley, the flowering trees become filled with blossoms, and the flowers that adorn the yards seem to all burst out at once.

Fatoumatou was thrilled to see the winter melt away and give way to warmer days. She loved being surrounded by the beauty of spring, and looked forward to seeing more of the sun. As the season progressed and summer drew closer, the temperatures in Boise started to climb, and by July, it was hot.

With the warmer temperatures, local agricultural jobs started to open up. This was a good time to look for field work. The IRC had informed Fatoumatou of work in the onion fields. She applied and was hired on.

The day before she was to report for work, Brother Pauline received a call from Blema. Unfortunately, he did not have good news.

"Brother Pauline, there's been an accident. Fatoumatou has been hurt. Would you please come to the hospital?"

Without hesitation, Brother and Sister Pauline hurried to meet him at Saint Alphonsus Hospital. When they arrived, they found him in the emergency room. Brother Pauline asked him what had happened.

"Fatoumatou was hit by a car," he explained. My car!"

"How in the world . . . ?" Brother Pauline asked, "How could this have happened?"

He and Sister Pauline looked at Blema in disbelief. To their knowledge, he did not own a car and did not drive. Blema led them to a quiet corner in the hospital where he could explain.

Wal-Mart was located about five miles from Blema's apartment, and he had been riding a bike to get to work each day. This had not been a problem in the spring, but as the temperatures climbed and the weather became hot, it became more and more of a challenge.

One day while at work, Blema talked with a coworker about his problem. His friend felt bad for him, and to be helpful, he generously offered him a car that he owned but was not using. Blema explained to him that he didn't know how to drive and didn't have a driver's license, but his friend expressed confidence that he would be able to learn quickly and obtain a license, and he encouraged him to take the car.

That evening his friend drove the older red car to Blema's apartment. Fatoumatou could hardly contain her excitement. The car was parked in a covered stall in front of the apartment. Blema came out and stood by the car with his friend as he pointed out its quirks and explained how to maintain it. Although the car had a stick shift, his friend believed that he would have no problem learning to drive it.

After Blema's friend had gone, Blema noticed that the car had been parked in the neighbor's stall. Not wanting to upset his neighbor, he decided to move it to the adjacent stall in front of their apartment.

Fatoumatou sat on the front step of their apartment and proudly watched as her husband backed up the car and maneuvered it out of the stall. He then turned the wheel and pointed the nose of the car toward the stall directly in front of their apartment door.

With the car lined up, Blema pressed on the gas pedal to move forward. The car did not respond. He pressed a bit harder. Suddenly, the car jumped forward, and rolled onto the step where Fatoumatou was sitting! Everything had happened so suddenly that Fatoumatou was unable to move out of the way in time. As she raised her arm to shield herself from the impact, her arm was struck by the bumper of the car and was shattered.

As Blema told the story, his voice was filled with emotion. He knew he had been responsible for the accident, and he did not want to leave Fatoumatou's side.

When Fatoumatou was released from the hospital a week later, her arm was held together with rods and pins. It would take several painful, difficult years to recover from the accident.

CHAPTER 23
The Pamphlet on the Wall

August rolled around quickly, accompanied by sultry nights, sugar beets, and the Western Idaho Fair. For Brother and Sister Pauline, August also meant that they were approaching the end of their mission at the employment center. They knew that it would be difficult for them to leave. They had enjoyed their mission and felt richly blessed by the friendships they had made in the time they were there. They hoped that these friendships would continue to be a part of their lives for years to come.

After they were released, they spent the next few weeks traveling to visit with family. When they returned, they felt a need to go and visit Blema and Fatoumatou.

When they arrived at the apartment and knocked on the door, no one answered. They knocked again. This time they heard Fatoumatou's faint voice, inviting them to come inside.

When Brother Pauline opened the door and they walked inside, they found Fatoumatou lying on the couch, alone and despondent. She had been struggling with complications from her injured arm. The pain and swelling had become so severe that it was almost more than she could bear.

Hurrying across the room, the Paulines rushed to her aid. They helped her into a semi-sitting position, propped up her arm with pillows and then covered it with ice packs.

Fatoumatou, they learned, had been suffering for weeks and had been unable to move far from the couch. During the day, she had lain immobile for hours all while Blema was away at work. The hours of solitude had added to her distress, and she had become very depressed.

The Paulines felt terrible. Over the next few days, they brought her ice packs for her swelling arm and made sure that her prescriptions for pain medication were filled. They found that the one thing that helped her most, however, was cherry cheesecake!

Stopping by one day, unannounced and bearing Fatoumatou's favorite desert, they were pleased to find Blema at home. As they walked into the room, they immediately noticed something different about the living room décor. The Joseph Smith pamphlet that Brother Pauline had given to Blema months before was now hanging in the center of their wall.

"Aahh, I see you have a new picture on your wall!" Brother Pauline teased.

Sister Pauline had noticed it too. "What a nice addition! We like it!"

Since Blema had not said anything about the Book of Mormon since the day they had given it to him, the Paulines had assumed that either he had not read it, or was not interested.

"Blema, have you been reading the Book of Mormon?" Brother Pauline asked.

"Yes, I've read most of it."

"Really?"

"Yes, I began reading it the day you gave it to me."

"That's wonderful! Well . . . what do you think?"

"Oh, this is a very important book!" Blema exclaimed. "It is truly a book from God!"

"Yes, it is," replied Brother Pauline.

Brother Pauline turned to Fatoumatou. "Has Blema been reading this book to you, Fatoumatou?" he asked in French.

"*Oui*," she answered.

"How do you feel about it?"

"I like it," she said in French. "It feels right."

The Paulines smiled, knowing exactly what she meant.

"Fatoumatou, can I share something with you?" asked Brother Pauline. "It's from the Book of Mormon."

Fatoumatou nodded.

Brother Pauline reached for the French copy of the book that was lying on a table. He opened it and began reading from Moroni 10:3–5.

"Behold, I would exhort you that when ye shall read these things, if it be wisdom in God that ye should read them, that ye would remember how merciful the Lord hath been unto the children of men, from the creation of Adam even down until the time that ye shall receive these things, and ponder it in your hearts.

"And when ye shall receive these things, I would exhort you that ye would ask God, the Eternal Father, in the name of Christ, if these things are not true; and if ye shall ask with a sincere heart, with real intent, having faith in Christ, he will manifest the truth of it unto you, by the power of the Holy Ghost.

"And by the power of the Holy Ghost ye may know the truth of all things."

"Isn't that is a wonderful promise?" asked Brother Pauline.

"*Oui*!"

"Fatoumatou, I know that if you will pray about this book, the Lord will let you know if it is true,"

Fatoumatou smiled, "*Oui, c'est bon*."

"Blema, do you have any questions?" Brother Pauline asked.

"Well . . . yes. I do have one question," Blema replied. "In the Book of Mormon, I've read of Abraham. Is this the same Abraham that's spoken of in the Bible?"

"Yes, it is. The ancient people that you've read about in the Book of Mormon knew and worshiped the same God of Abraham, Isaac, and Jacob, as we know from the Bible."

Brother Pauline proceeded to tell Blema how Joseph Smith had been able to obtain the records of these people and translate them into English through the direction given to him by the Lord.

Blema picked up the Book of Mormon and held it in his hands. "I believe that what you are telling me is true," he said, "but there's something that troubles me."

"Oh, what's that?"

"Well, if this book is truly from God, why don't they know about it in Africa?"

"They do, Blema. As you know, Africa is a big place with many restrictive governments and religions. Because of this, the Church has not been able to reach all parts of Africa. In Ghana, the Church is well established, and there's even a temple there, but in some countries the governments have restricted Christianity and have not allowed the missionaries to freely come in and teach their message.

"Yes, I know that's true," Blema agreed.

"We need to pray that those countries will open up and allow the gospel to be taught there so all people will have the truths of this book that we hold in our hands.

"Blema," Brother Pauline continued, "there's so much that we want to share with you and Fatoumatou. There's so much truth that's been revealed in this book, I just want to share it all with you right now, but of course, I know that's impossible. We all have to learn things 'line upon line, precept upon precept', a little at a time. Would you and Fatoumatou be interested in having the missionaries come and speak to you and start teaching you some of these truths?"

Blema turned to Fatoumatou, asking her in French. He then turned back to Brother Pauline. "Oh yes," he said. "We would like that very much. Thank you. *C'est tres bon.*"

CHAPTER 24
Meeting the Missionaries

Elder Moose and Elder Hopkins were the first of several missionaries assigned to teach Blema and Fatoumatou. When Brother Pauline had called the Boise mission office to arrange for someone to teach them, he was assured that they would be sending two of the finest missionaries in the area.

"Great!" he replied. "Does either of them speak French?"

"I don't believe so. Why?"

"Well, Fatoumatou speaks very little English. It would be a shame if she weren't able to participate in the discussions. I speak a little French, but it's limited and doesn't include gospel-oriented vocabulary. I think it's important for us to find someone who can speak well enough to interpret."

"I see. I don't know of anyone offhand, but I'll certainly see what we can come up with. I'm afraid I can't guarantee anything though."

Several days later, Brother Pauline received a report from the mission office that several people had been found who spoke French. Unfortunately, none spoke well enough to translate.

Not content to stand by and wait, Elder Moose and Elder Hopkins began their own search. One day, while meeting with the ward mission leader of the Columbus Park Ward, Brother Briscoe, they told him of the dilemma.

"We have some good news and some bad news." Elder Hopkins told him. "The good news is that we have been assigned to teach a couple from West Africa who are living in your ward boundaries." He then continued, "The bad news is, we are unable to find anyone who knows French well enough to interpret for us. You wouldn't know of anyone would you?"

"Well, as a matter of fact, I do," he replied. "My wife, Christine, speaks fluent French. I'm sure that she would love to interpret for you. She's always looking for opportunities to bone up on her language skills."

Sister Briscoe was thrilled when she received the invitation. In mid-October, she joined the missionaries at the Fangamous' apartment for their first discussion.

Elder Hopkins and Elder Moose were excited to have the opportunity to teach Blema and Fatoumatou the gospel. Both missionaries had a strong testimony of the gospel's truthfulness, and they felt a desire to share their message with anyone who was prepared to listen. It was for this very purpose that they had left their homes and families for two years. From the time they met Blema and Fatoumatou, they felt good about them. Because of the couple's humility and desire to know truth, they felt that they were ready to be taught.

As the first discussion commenced, a prayer was said to invite the Spirit. The scriptures were opened, and the missionaries began to teach Blema and Fatoumatou the plan of salvation.

"The Lord, Jesus Christ has come to earth to show us the way back to our Heavenly Father," they taught. "He gave His life so that we, through Him, might have eternal life. He has also provided a way for us to be with our families forever." Christine listened as the Elders taught and then repeated their words in French.

After teaching each new principle, the missionaries asked Blema and Fatoumatou if they had understood what was being taught. Blema would often reply that he had, and then follow up by offering a beautifully worded, in depth explanation of *why* he believed it were true. When Fatoumatou had a question, it was often Blema that provided her with the answer.

The elders and Sister Briscoe came to Blema and Fatoumatou's home every week for several weeks. Each time they met, they enjoyed a wonderful feast of the Spirit as Blema and Fatoumatou were taught new gospel principles.

The meetings continued until the day that Elder Hopkins and Elder Moose received some sad news. They would be transferred to a new location and wouldn't be able to continue with the lessons. Blema and Fatoumatou felt disappointed, but the elders assured them that they would be in good hands as Elder Ludwig and Elder Bowers would be taking their place.

Elder Ludwig and Elder Bowers were pleased to meet Blema and Fatoumatou and were immediately impressed by their eagerness to be taught the gospel. The elders were excited to begin teaching them, and they took up the lessons where Elder Hopkins and Elder Moose had left off. Sister Briscoe continued to come and interpret for them.

One of the first lessons the new missionaries taught was on the principle of tithing. They began the lesson by quoting Malachi 3:10.

"Bring ye all the tithes into the storehouse, that there may be meat in mine house, and prove me now herewith, saith the Lord of hosts, if I will not open you the windows of heaven, and pour you out a blessing that there shall not be room enough to receive it."

"Isn't this a great blessing?" asked Elder Bowers. "Many of the principles of the gospel are given with a promise. When the Lord gives us a commandment, He expects us to follow it. If we are obedient, He rewards us by pouring out His blessings in such great abundance, that at times, it seems hard to receive them all."

Blema and Fatoumatou listened carefully as the elders presented the lesson. Blema was deeply impressed by their comments, remembering the covenant that he had already made with the Lord to pay his tithe.

On another day, the elders presented a lesson that was on the Word of Wisdom, a revelation and guideline for good physical health that was given to Joseph Smith and then recorded in the eighty-ninth section of the Doctrine and Covenants. Once again, Sister Briscoe was there to interpret for them.

"It is important to keep our bodies free from all harmful substances, especially those that will alter our state of mind," Elder Ludwig taught. "When we follow these guidelines, not only will we enjoy a greater degree of health, but we will be more open to the influence of the Spirit of God."

Blema and Fatoumatou listened as the elders took turns presenting the lesson.

"That's right," Elder Bowers confirmed. "The Word of Wisdom is another principle with a promise. We are told in D&C 89:18–21, that 'all saints who remember to keep and do these sayings, walking in obedience to the commandments, shall receive health in their navel and marrow to their bones; and shall find wisdom and great treasures of knowledge, even hidden treasures; and shall run and not be weary, and shall walk and not faint.' Isn't that a wonderful promise?"

"Yes, it is," agreed Blema and Fatoumatou.

"What are we supposed to eat then?" Fatoumatou asked.

"That's a good question, Fatoumatou. The Lord has placed many things on the earth that are good for us to eat and will make us healthy. He has shown us that all wholesome grains and herbs are good for our bodies. Vegetables, and the 'fruit of the vine,' are good for us as well. The 'flesh of beasts and fowls of the air,' or different kinds of meat and fish are also given for our use, but are to be eaten sparingly."

"That sounds good," said Fatoumatou. "Those are the things that we're eating already."

"Very good," Elder Ludwig said.

"There are also certain things that we should try to avoid," he continued. "We are told that we should not partake of 'strong drink,' nor alcohol. We are taught that alcohol was given to us for the washing of our bodies, and not for our consumption. We are also taught that tobacco is not good for us, as well as 'hot drinks.' This has been interpreted to mean coffee or tea.

Fatoumatou turned to Blema. "If we are to be baptized," she said, "we will do everything the Lord asks of us!"

Blema thought about what she said, and after a short hesitation, motioned for the missionaries to follow him into the kitchen. The missionaries stood in the kitchen and watched as he opened up the cupboard door and took out a container of Nesquik, holding it up for them to see. "Is this okay?" he asked.

The elders exchanged smiles and told Blema, "Yes, hot chocolate is fine."

Again Blema reached into the cupboard and pulled out some tea. "Is this okay?"

The Elders checked the tea and found that it was black tea and contained caffeine. "No, I'm sorry. Herb teas are fine, but this tea is not."

Blema handed the box of tea to the elders, and then went back to the cupboard. Pulling out a large can of coffee, he looked down at it as though he were about to lose a good friend. "Is this okay?" he asked, knowing what the answer would be.

"No, I'm afraid not," answered Elder Ludwig.

Blema lowered his head as he held it out for them to take. With a look of resignation, he said, "Here, take it!"

Blema continued to go through his cupboards until the Elders arms were filled with cans and boxes.

When the discussion had ended, the elders and Sister Briscoe said their "good-byes" and got up to leave. They had shut the door behind them, and had only taken a few steps, when suddenly, the door swung open once again.

"Hey!" Fatoumatou called out. When they turned around, they saw her standing at the doorway holding out one more box of tea. Everyone laughed with delight, touched by this simple act of faith.

CHAPTER 25
A Seed of Faith

Through their discussions with the missionaries, Blema and Fatoumatou had gained a testimony of the truthfulness of the gospel and of the Restored Church, and they had a strong desire to enter the waters of baptism. Unfortunately, there was something holding them back. Before they could be baptized, they were required to attend sacrament meeting on Sunday. Because Blema's work schedule demanded that he work on Sundays almost every week, they hadn't been to church yet. Although several efforts had been made to have the schedule changed, these efforts had been unsuccessful.

Blema was tempted to approach his manager one more time and ask him for the day off, but it seemed like a bad time to push the issue. Wal-Mart had already laid off several of their employees because of the sluggish economy, and he knew that his position was vulnerable.

Voicing his frustrations over the situation to Brother Pauline one day, Blema asked him what he should do.

"Be patient, Blema," Brother Pauline admonished. "The Lord knows your heart, and he knows of your desires to be baptized. He'll prepare a way for you to attend church. Just be faithful and it will happen."

Blema tried to take this counsel to heart, but it was difficult. When he prayed about the matter, he received no clear answers. Fatoumatou had been offering up prayers of her own, and she felt that she knew what they needed to do.

"Blema, when we were in the camp and were faced with problems that we couldn't solve, we fasted and prayed. While we were in the camp I promised the Lord that I would fast for two months after we were resettled to show my gratitude. I believe it's time to keep my promise."

That day, Fatoumatou began to fast, and Blema joined her. They skipped their breakfast and then went all day without food or drink, eating only a simple meal at night. This continued for several days as they poured out their hearts in prayer, asking the Lord to provide a way for them to be baptized.

Day after day went by, and it seemed to them that their prayers were going unanswered. Still, they continued to fast and pray.

After a couple of weeks had gone by, Blema went to work one morning as usual. As he entered the store, he was told that the supervisor had asked to speak with him. Afraid that he was about to lose his job, Blema's heart began to pound as he made his way to the supervisor's office.

"Hello, Blema," said the supervisor. "Please, have a seat."

"Thank you, sir."

"Blema, do you know why I've asked to speak with you today?"

"No, sir."

"Well, first of all, on behalf of Wal-Mart, I would like to thank you for all of your hard work."

Blema shifted in his seat. Although he tried to appear calm, he was trembling inside, afraid of what was to come next.

"Because you have been such a dedicated employee," he continued, "we've decided to increase your wages and give you Sundays off."

Blema stared ahead in a daze of disbelief. Suddenly, a broad smile swept over his face.

"No, you haven't!" he exclaimed.

The supervisor looked at him and wondered if he had understood him correctly. Just to make sure, he repeated his statement.

"Yes, Blema, we've decided to increase your wages and give you Sundays off!"

"No, you haven't!" Blema declared again. "The Lord has done it!"

The supervisor smiled. "Okay, Blema . . . . congratulations."

Fatoumatou was overjoyed when she heard the news, knowing that this had been an answer to their prayers. Although Blema ended his fast, she continued fasting until she had done so for two months, fulfilling the vow she had made in the camp.

* * * * *

Blema and Fatoumatou were looking forward to attending church. On Blema's first Sunday off, Brother and Sister Briscoe picked them up, and together they went to the Columbus Park Ward off of Vista Avenue. As they approached the building, Blema and Fatoumatou looked out of the car window to get their first view of the church, an older building with red brick construction. The church grounds were green and neatly kept, and the parking lot was already filling up with cars.

Fatoumatou took Blema's arm as they walked inside. Following the Briscoes into the chapel, Blema and Fatoumatou took their seats on a long padded bench. Fatoumatou sat next to Sister Briscoe, who would interpret the meeting for her. This put Fatoumatou at ease. She liked Sister Briscoe, and it was good to have her there.

Blema looked around the room as people came in and took their seats. He noticed that all of the men were dressed in white shirts and ties, and it sparked the memory of a white shirt he had worn in Africa. Soon, organ music began to play.

As the services began, Blema and Fatoumatou relaxed. They could feel a calm and reassuring spirit fill the room, and somehow, they felt as if they had come home. They knew in their hearts that this is where they needed to be.

In the weeks that followed, they continued to attend church every Sunday. After several weeks, Bishop Fisher called them into his office to speak with them. He told them that he had been pleased by their faithfulness and then gave his approval for them to be baptized. Blema and Fatoumatou were overjoyed. Elder Bowers and Elder Ludwig would make the arrangements.

At Blema's request, the elders called Brother Pauline to ask if he would perform the baptism.

"It would be an honor and a privilege," Brother Pauline told them.

Sister Pauline was thrilled. The baptism was scheduled to be performed in two weeks.

* * * * *

While Blema and Fatoumatou were awaiting the day of their baptism, they were informed by the housing authorities that they had finally been approved for subsidized housing. They would now be able to move into a new apartment with a lower rent.

The new apartment was located closer to downtown—on 13th Street. This would place Blema and Fatoumatou within a different church ward boundary. For them, this meant that they would be leaving the ward that they had become familiar with and would attend the Boise 13th Ward after the move.

When Bishop Conrad Stevens learned that Blema and Fatoumatou were moving into his ward, he asked Brother Ladwig, the elder's quorum president, if he would mind rounding up some of their ward members and help with the move. Brother Ladwig was more than happy to do it.

It was early Saturday morning when Brother Ladwig pulled up to Blema and Fatoumatou's apartment in a big truck. He had only just arrived when other volunteers began to appear. With everyone working together, the move went quickly. Within just a couple of hours, the truck had been loaded with boxes and furniture, driven across town, unloaded, and stacked in the living room of the new apartment. Blema and Fatoumatou were amazed and extremely grateful for the service that was provided for them that day. It was hard for them to believe that people they didn't even know had been so willing to help.

Now, with the move behind them, they could focus on preparing themselves for the baptism that was to take place the following week.

CHAPTER 26
Mormons Eat People

"There is no good deed that goes unpunished," or so the saying goes, and truly, nothing is done to further the work of the Lord without Satan standing by to frustrate our well-intentioned plans.

The baptism had been set for Friday, March 21, 2010, and everything seemed to be in order. On the Tuesday before the baptism, Brother and Sister Pauline went to Blema and Fatoumatou's new apartment to pay them a visit.

"Well, are you ready for Friday?" Brother Pauline asked, expecting an enthusiastic response, but there was no answer. Blema's eyes were on Fatoumatou as she looked at the floor with a blank stare.

"Is there a problem?" Brother Pauline asked.

"Fatoumatou feels that Friday might not be a good day for the baptism." Blema replied. "She thinks it might be best to wait."

Brother and Sister Pauline were surprised, knowing how excited she had been just days before. She and Blema had spent much time fasting and praying in preparation for their baptism.

"Why do you feel that way, Fatoumatou?" Brother Pauline asked. He spoke in English while Blema interpreted for him. Blema repeated the question to Fatoumatou in French and then waited for her response.

Fatoumatou's broad shoulders slumped as she answered Blema in Mandinka. Blema listened, and then looked up, shocked by what she had said.

"Fatoumatou tells me that she spoke to Kafui about the baptism, and she warned her not to go through with it. Kafui told her that Mormons kill people and eat their flesh."

Brother and Sister Pauline stared at him in disbelief.

"Fatoumatou," said Brother Pauline, "do you believe that's true?"

Fatoumatou continued to stare at the floor.

"When you prayed about the baptism, can you remember how it made you feel? The Lord communicates with us through the Holy Ghost, and when we are doing the things that are right, we will feel peace in our hearts and in our minds."

After a long pause of silence, Brother Pauline continued, "Look, Fatoumatou, I know that this is a big step for you, but I want to reassure you that what you are doing is right. I know that the Spirit has testified to you that the things that you have learned concerning this gospel are true. The Lord desires for you to be baptized."

Fatoumatou lifted her head and looked at Brother Pauline as he spoke.

"Of course, you can take all the time you need to feel good about your decision. I want you to know that you have a lot of people that are supporting you."

Fatoumatou relaxed as she thought of the feelings of calm reassurance that she had felt so many times as she had been taught by the missionaries. It was the same warm feeling that had accompanied her prayers.

After much thought, she sat up straight and squared her shoulders. "You're right." She declared. "I want to be baptized. We will do it on Friday."

CHAPTER 27
The Baptism

THE BIG DAY HAD FINALLY ARRIVED. ON FRIDAY EVENING, MARCH 21, 2010, Brother and Sister Pauline went early to pick up Blema and Fatoumatou to take them to the Columbus Ward church building. When they got to the apartment, Fatoumatou was waiting at the door, dressed in her Sunday best.

"You look beautiful, Fatoumatou," Sister Pauline exclaimed. "I'm glad to see you smiling!"

Fatoumatou laughed. "I am very happy today!" she said.

"We're both happy today," Blema added. "We have waited for this day for a long time!"

"You certainly have," agreed Brother Pauline. "This is a wonderful day! Thank you for letting us share it with you."

When they arrived at the church building, Elder Bowers and Elder Ludwig were there to greet them. The elders had been there for over an hour. They had filled the font with water and set up chairs, making sure everything was ready.

"Blema! Fatoumatou! We're so happy to see you." Elder Bowers said when he saw them come through the door.

"Aahh, yes! There they are!" said Elder Ludwig. "We're glad you're here. We've been looking forward to this all day. Do you feel that you're ready for this?"

"Oh, yes!" replied Blema. Fatoumatou smiled and nodded.

With a few last instructions, Blema and Fatoumatou were ushered to the dressing rooms where they were given white clothes to be baptized in. The missionaries explained the significance of the clothing. "White represents purity," they said. "You will also be pure when your sins have been washed away."

While Blema and Fatoumatou were getting dressed, the missionaries greeted others as they arrived. The thirty chairs that the elders had set up in front of the font were quickly filled. Before long they realized that there wasn't going be enough chairs to seat everyone, and it was decided that the meeting would be moved to the chapel where there would be more room.

When Blema and Fatoumatou finally stepped out of the dressing room and into the chapel, they were surprised to see all of the people that had come. Bishop Stevens of the 13th Ward, his first councilor, Brother Jerry Sturgill, and the Briscoes of the Columbus Park ward were all there, as well as other members from the 13th, Columbus Park, and Autumn Fair wards. Even Kakou and Kafui had come, dressed in their brightly colored African clothing.

Blema and Fatoumatou followed the elders as they led them to their seats on the front pew in the chapel, and the elders took their seats beside them. Brother Briscoe, who would be conducting the meeting, stood behind the pulpit and waited for them to take their seats.

"We would like to welcome all of you on this special occasion," he said, when everyone was seated. "Blema and Fatoumatou have waited a long time for this day, and it's a great joy for us to be able to share it with them."

Brother Christensen had been asked to speak about the importance of baptism. When he got up to speak, he talked of the sacred covenants that Blema and Fatoumatou would be entering into that day. Blema and Fatoumatou sat attentively as he spoke, listening to every word as he alternated his message between French and English.

When he had finished, Sister Briscoe stood and sang, "When I Am Baptized," in French. Fatoumatou was touched to hear her sing the beautiful words in her own language.

Then it was time for the baptisms. Brother Pauline motioned for Blema to follow him into the font. When they had stepped into the clear, warm water, Blema placed his hand on Brother Pauline's forearm in the way he had been shown. Brother Pauline looked at Blema and smiled. "Blema Fangamou," he said with a clear voice, "Having been commissioned of Jesus Christ, I baptize you in the name of the Father, and of the Son, and of the Holy Ghost. Amen."

Brother Pauline then laid Blema down in the water, immersing him completely. When he came up again, he wiped the water from his eyes and grinned. His face seemed to glow with joy. Brother Pauline gave Blema's shoulder a congratulatory squeeze, and the men embraced.

Fatoumatou was next. She moved forward, taking slow steps into the water so she wouldn't fall. Brother Pauline held his hand out to help her in. Fatoumatou smiled. Brother Pauline placed her hand on his arm, and showed her how to hold her nose with the other. "Fatoumatou Diallo," he began, and then repeated the baptismal prayer. When he tried to immerse her in the water, he couldn't get a good hold on her. Most of her body went down into the water, but the top part of her head remained dry. It was apparent that he would need some help.

Brother Pauline motioned for Blema to come closer. After a brief collaboration, they had come up with a plan. Brother Pauline tried again. "Fatoumatou Diallo," he said, then proceeding with the prayer. Before he could say "amen," Blema had come down into the water behind Fatoumatou, taking hold of her shoulders and gently pulling her down into the water. The witnesses smiled and nodded, indicating the baptism had been properly performed. Fatoumatou came up beaming. "*Merci*!"she exclaimed.

Blema and Fatoumatou changed back into their dry clothing and joined the others back in the chapel where Elder Ludwig gave a wonderful talk on the Holy Ghost. After saying a few words, Bishop Fisher invited everyone into the cultural hall for refreshments.

The baptism had indeed been a joyous occasion. There wasn't one soul among all those who had witnessed this wonderful event that didn't feel that their lives had been blessed that day.

CHAPTER 28
The Dream

TWICE A YEAR, THE CHURCH OF JESUS CHRIST OF LATTER-DAY Saints holds a general conference. For two days during the conference, the leaders of the Church address the members, giving them direction and edification. The meetings are broadcast over television and radio in many areas of the northwest and other parts of the United States. The conference can also be seen through satellite in many church buildings throughout the world. The next general conference was to be held on April 3–4, 2010, two weeks after Blema and Fatoumatou's baptism.

Blema and Fatoumatou were excited about the conference and had a desire to hear the Prophet and Apostles address the church. They had told Brother Pauline of their desires. Brother Pauline wanted this for them as well, so he called Bishop Stevens to make arrangements for them to watch the conference in French through satellite in the 13th Ward church building. Bishop Stevens assured him that accommodations would be made.

On Saturday morning, the day of the conference, Brother and Sister Pauline went to pick up Blema and Fatoumatou to take them to the church. They had dressed in their best church clothing; Blema in a white shirt and tie, while Fatoumatou wore a beautiful, colorful African skirt.

On the way to the church, Blema and Fatoumatou sat in the backseat of the car and spoke to the Pauline's about their recent baptism, recounting the blessings that had recently come to them. They expressed their excitement over being able to listen to general conference and of being able to see the Prophet for the first time. They were also looking forward to seeing their new ward building where they would be worshipping from now on.

The pleasant chatter continued as the car turned the corner onto Bogus Basin Road. When they had gone just a short distance, the road began to ascend up a hill, and as the car climbed, the church building suddenly came into view. Blema grew quiet.

"Blema, are you all right?" Sister Pauline asked, noticing his sudden withdrawal.

"Oh, yes." Blema replied. "I'm fine." Pointing up at the building, he quietly exclaimed, "I've seen this building before . . . in a dream!"

CHAPTER 29
A Vexed Heart

"WELL, BLEMA, ARE YOU HAPPY?" BROTHER PAULINE ASKED one day as he and his wife sat visiting with Blema and Fatoumatou in their home.

Blema beamed. "Oh yes. We are very happy. We have the gospel of Jesus Christ!"

"Isn't that wonderful!" exclaimed Sister Pauline. "We're so happy for you."

Blema sat next to Fatoumatou on the sofa. Fatoumatou forced a smile, but there was sadness in her eyes. Blema looked at her, and then he too became more somber.

"There is only one thing that vexes our hearts," he said.

"Oh? What is that?" asked Brother Pauline.

"We have not seen our children now for over twelve years. It's difficult to be happy when we know that they are suffering. It's hard to know that we might not ever see them again."

"I'm so sorry, Blema. Have you considered going to the immigration office to see if there is anything that can be done to bring them here?"

"Oh, yes. I've gone many times! I've given them our papers and they've promised to call, but we haven't heard anything. When I call, they can't tell me anything. I can't seem to get anywhere with them."

"Well, I think the most important thing is to not give up. Perhaps if we went together, we could get some answers. Would you like me to go to the office with you?"

"Yes, I would like that very much! Thank you."

The next day, Blema called the immigration office and made an appointment with Terri MacDonald at the Agency for New Americans. The appointment was set for April 7th. Brother Pauline picked up Blema a half hour early and took him there.

When they arrived, Terri MacDonald was not prepared to meet them. Somewhere along the line, their wires had been crossed and she did not have them on her schedule. After seeing the disappointment on Blema's face when she told him of the mistake, she agreed to try to squeeze him in. Blema and Brother Pauline thanked her for her kindness and followed her into her office.

After Blema and Brother Pauline had introduced themselves to Terri, Brother Pauline helped Blema to explain why they had come. Blema had placed an application with the agency months before, and that he not heard anything. He had come to find out the status of his application.

Terri nodded. "I see," she said. "Well, let's find out what's happening." She turned to her computer and typed in the information Blema had given her and then waited until his case file appeared on the screen.

After reading over the information, Terri turned to Blema. "I know that you're anxious to hear something," she said, "but I'm afraid that right now everything is out of our hands. We have sent your application to the US Citizenship and Immigration Service Center, and we are now waiting to hear from them. There isn't anything we can do until we receive their letter. When we receive it, we will call you and let you know."

Blema was disappointed but thanked her for her efforts.

When they had left the office, Brother Pauline turned to Blema, wanting to offer some encouragement. "Well, Blema," he said, "now at least we know the immigration center has received your application. We'll just have to be patient and hope that the letter will come quickly."

Within a week, Blema received a call from Terri, telling him that the letter had arrived. She requested that he and Brother Pauline come back to the office, and she would go over it with them.

Although they hoped that the letter contained positive news, when

Brother Pauline and Blema approached Terri at her office, her expression told them otherwise. After greeting them, Terri introduced them to Rabuel, one of the staff members who had been appointed to interpret the meeting in French. Since Blema had become proficient in English, both he and Brother Pauline felt that the presence of an interpreter was not a good sign.

Terri began by reading the letter out loud. In short, the letter was one of rejection. It noted discrepancies between the interview form that he had filled out while in the Kpomasse camp and the one that had been most recently received by the US Citizenship and Immigration Service Center. It stated that there were many other issues that needed to be resolved. First of all, there were no official documents to confirm the names of the children and establish their dates of birth. Because all of the children had been born at home, there were no birth certificates. To add to the confusion, two of the children's names had been changed by Fatoumatou's brother who had cared for them, and their names were different than those declared on the latest form. More evidence would be needed to support the application.

Blema sat up straight in his chair. He assured Terri that there was an explanation for all of the discrepancies. There was also a good reason for the way he had filled out the forms in Kpomasse. The situation that he had found himself in while in the camp required him to make certain statements that, although they were true, were incomplete. He asserted that he had been open about the declarations from the beginning.

"I'm sorry, Blema," said Terri, "but we will no longer be able to help you. I'm afraid that your case will require the services of an immigration attorney. I have a list of four attorneys in the Boise area that you can contact if you choose to pursue the immigrations on your own, but it could be costly. If you proceed, you will need to gather as much evidence as you can. The immigration agency is not requiring DNA tests; however, they have advised that the tests could be critical in verifying parentage. These tests could cost over twelve hundred dollars for the four children, and you will have to meet a deadline. All evidence must be submitted by June twenty-ninth, or the case will be deemed closed. No extensions will be permitted."

The news hit Blema hard. He felt devastated. It was as if every ounce of hope within him had been instantly ripped away. He knew that he would not be able to afford the services of an attorney, nor could he afford the fee for the DNA tests. A few thousand dollars might as well be a few million. The reality of the situation was that he would most likely never see his children again. He pushed away the thought to keep from getting overly emotional.

By the time Brother Pauline and Blema left the office, Blema's disappointment and frustration had turned to anger. "These people are talking like they knew nothing about the way the children were declared on the forms," he exclaimed. "I told them all of this when we first started the application process. They have known it all along, and now they are talking to me like this? They know I don't have money for an attorney. And how am I supposed to come up with twelve hundred dollars for DNA tests? Oh, Lord, what am I going to do?"

"Blema, I know that you're upset. I don't know why the agency was so quick to dismiss your case. It could just be that they're overwhelmed by the number of cases waiting to be processed, and they can't deal with any case that's not cut and dry. I'm sorry."

Blema went silent and stared ahead. After a long pause, he asked, "What am I going to tell Fatoumatou? How can I tell the children?"

"Blema, listen. The most important thing is that we don't lose hope. The Lord loves you, and if it is His will, He will provide a way for you and your children to be reunited. I know that you and Fatoumatou have seen many miracles in the past. We need to ask him for one more."

"I know that's true," Blema said, "but there's no way that I can afford an attorney. It's too much. We're barely getting by as it is."

"Blema, the Lord is going to provide. We don't need to worry about where the money is going to come from. You're paying your tithing and keeping the commandments, aren't you?"

"Yes."

"Then if He wants those children here, they will be. He will provide the money for the attorney and for the DNA tests. We just need to trust Him."

When they had arrived at the apartment, at Blema's request, Brother Pauline followed him in to help break the news to Fatoumatou.

Fatoumatou knew when she saw Blema that she was about to hear bad news. When he told her what had happened, it was more than she could bear. Suddenly, her body felt heavy. She made her way across the room and fell onto the sofa. Blema followed her and sat beside her, stroking her arm while Brother Pauline spoke.

"We can't give up hope, Fatoumatou," he said. "We need to trust that the Lord will provide a way to bring your children here. We serve a mighty God, and if it is His will, they will come!"

CHAPTER 30
After All We Can Do

Brother Pauline had spent his career in government, retiring as an administrative analyst for city, county, and state government agencies in the state of California. He hoped that his experience in assessing complex legislation and preparing summaries of regulations might prove to be useful in helping Blema and Fatoumatou with their dilemma.

After some thought as to how they should proceed, he took it upon himself to get things moving. He asked Blema for the files that had been given to him by the US Citizenship and Immigration Service Center. He would use them to prepare a document to summarize Blema's case. He felt that if he did most of the preliminary work before presenting it to an attorney, they might have a better chance at finding someone to take the case.

After reading and assessing each child's case file, Brother Pauline wrote up a summary and drafted an open letter to solicit the assistance of an attorney. He sent these documents to Brother Stephen Ladwig, the elders quorum president in Blema's ward, asking him if he knew any of the attorneys on the list that had been provided them. Brother Ladwig stated that he didn't, but that he would share the documents with Bishop Stevens and his counselors at a ward council meeting.

On April 19th, Brother Sturgill, first counselor in the bishopric, read the letter and was intrigued by it. He had already developed a soft spot for this sweet African couple who had moved into his ward just weeks before. He had attended Blema and Fatoumatou's baptism and was touched by the uniqueness of their situation.

Having served a mission in Canada where he learned to speak French, Brother Sturgill was able to communicate freely with both Blema and Fatoumatou. He felt a special connection with them and had a desire to support them as they began their journey as members of the Church. When they moved into his ward, he had made a special effort to see that they were receiving the benefits of learning the gospel in the language that they were most familiar. He had also been instrumental in providing a way for them to watch the general conference in French through satellite, and he made sure that an interpreter was available for Fatoumatou when she attended the regular Sunday meetings.

After reading the letter, Brother Sturgill did not hesitate to call Brother Pauline to offer his assistance.

Brother Pauline remembered meeting Brother Sturgill at Blema and Fatoumatou's baptism, and he was happy to hear from him. He thanked him for his call and proceeded to tell him the reason for the letter.

"Have you had a chance to hear Blema and Fatoumatou's story?" he asked.

"Not really. I know that they came here as refugees. I don't know the details."

Brother Pauline quickly told Brother Sturgill a summarized version of Blema and Fatoumatou's story, and how they had been sadly separated from their children. "If we don't help them now," he said, "the chances are slim that they'll ever see their children again. I know that we'll be facing some big challenges if we're to move forward on this, but I feel like we need to try."

Brother Sturgill listened intently as Brother Pauline explained the situation. "I had no idea of what they'd been through," he said with concern. "It's a shame that they've been separated from their children for so long. I'll certainly do all that I can to help. Just let me know what I can do."

"Well, I'm just trying to figure it out myself. I feel that the Lord's hand is in this, and I'm praying that He will guide me along the way. My knowledge and experience in legal matters is limited, and I know even less about immigration. I know that if we're going to proceed with this, we'll need to find an attorney. You wouldn't happen to know any of the attorneys on the list, would you?"

"No, I'm afraid I don't," said Brother Sturgill. "I am an attorney, but I haven't worked specifically with immigration issues. My wife, Christine, was involved with assisting students at Brigham Young University with immigration, however. She may know of someone, or maybe we could check with the BYU alumni association. I'll certainly look into it and see what I can do."

"Oh, that would be wonderful. Before you do that though, there's something else you need to know. I hate to say this, but the biggest challenge isn't going to be finding an attorney to work on the case, but in finding one who's willing to work without pay. Blema and Fatoumatou are just barely getting by as it is, and they won't be able to pay an attorney. It might sound crazy, but I believe that if the Lord wants those children here, there'll be someone out there who is willing to take this on."

"Well, that certainly does make it more challenging, but I think that you're absolutely right. I don't know what the chances are of finding someone here in Boise though. We may have to search some of the bigger cities, New York or Los Angeles, or somewhere where immigration is more common. "

"Yes, well, I'm certainly willing to do that if it's necessary. I think that before we approach an attorney though, we should do as much of the staff work as possible. That would minimize the time that they would have to spend on the case.

"I agree."

"I'm thinking that the first thing we need to do is address the request for evidence issues that has been raised by immigration. They will want to have proof that these children truly belong to Blema and Fatoumatou. Unfortunately, that might require DNA tests from all the children, which could be expensive and difficult to obtain. The children are in Labe with Fatoumatou's brother, and they'll have to travel to Guinea-Conakry to take the tests. I think that's about 250 miles from Labe. I guess we'll have to figure all of that out when we get to it."

"Sounds like this is going to be a huge undertaking, Brother Pauline. I do think that it's definitely a worthwhile endeavor, though. Blema and Fatoumatou are good people, and I believe the Lord wants their family to be together. I'm willing to work with you to try to make that happen. Is there anything I can do right now?"

"Well, I've already begun some of the preliminary work. If you don't mind, I would like to email you a copy of what I have already prepared and have you look over it to see if it meets up with legal requirements."

"I'd be glad to do that. I'll get back to you if I'm able to find anything out about an immigration attorney."

"Thank you, Brother. Oh, one more thing. We have a deadline. The packet will have to be in the hands of Immigration no later than June twenty-ninth."

Brother Sturgill wasted no time getting started. That very day he began a search for an attorney, and by the end of the week, after many inquiries, he had found David Purnell, an immigration attorney in Boise, Idaho.

David Purnell was also a member of the Church and had learned to speak French while on a mission to France. After reading a summary of the case that Brother Sturgill sent to him, he was touched by Blema and Fatoumatou's story, and he agreed to take on the case—pro bono!

* * * * *

When Brother and Sister Pauline went to Wal-Mart to tell Blema the good news, they found him arranging bananas in the produce aisle.

"Blema, is it possible for you to take a break? There's something we need to tell you."

Blema's face showed concern. "Well, I believe so. I'll go ask."

"Okay. We'll wait for you."

After several minutes, Blema returned without his apron.

"What is it?" he asked. "Is there a problem?"

"No, Blema, there's no problem. We have some good news!"

"Oh?"

"Remember how we prayed to find an attorney to handle your case? Well, our prayers have been answered. We now have an attorney! His name is David Purnell, and he lives here in Boise. He's a member of our church, and he speaks French. And guess what, Blema? He's going to work for free!"

Blema's eyes grew wide as he listened. Without a word, he turned around and began to run as fast as he could down the aisle toward the back of the store. Brother and Sister Pauline stood, stunned by his sudden display of emotion, not knowing quite what to do. They were somewhat embarrassed, but even more delighted, as they watched him run all the way to the end of the aisle, turn around, and come dancing and singing all the way back to where they were standing.

"Oh, praise the Lord!" he beamed. "That's wonderful news! I am very, very happy today!"

On May 5th, following directions to an address they had been given, Blema, Brother Sturgill, and Brother Pauline made their way to the twelfth floor of the US Bank building in downtown Boise where they met Brother Purnell for the first time. They met in a conference room that overlooked the city.

"Hello, Blema!" Brother Purnell greeted warmly. "It's very good to meet you. I've heard so much about you."

"And it's good to meet you." Blema replied. "Fatoumatou and I would like to thank you for helping us!"

"It's my pleasure, Blema. It sounds like we have our work cut out for us."

"Yes."

"Well, why don't we start at the beginning? Tell me what you've done so far."

Speaking in French, Blema described his case to Brother Purnell. Brother Sturgill and Brother Pauline listened and filled in where it was necessary. Brother Sturgill handed Brother Purnell a copy of the revisions of the first draft response, while Brother Pauline assured him that they would try to do as much of any future paperwork as possible. He proposed writing up the drafts and then submitting them to him for his final approval, helping him to fit the case into his busy workload. Brother Purnell agreed. They all knew that the case would require them to work as a team.

When the men had left the conference room, Brother Purnell began working on the case right away. He submitted the required documents to the US Immigration Agency so he would be recognized as Blema's attorney on record. This would allow him access to the file and other documents related to the case. There were now just seven more weeks until the deadline.

Up to this point, Blema had been hesitant to share any information about their efforts with the children, afraid that they would get their hopes up only to have them dashed. After meeting with Brother Purnell however, Blema was beginning to feel a real sense of hope, and he couldn't wait to share it with his children. He called them as soon as he had returned home.

"Hello, Joseph?"

"Yes, Father! How are you today?"

"I am doing well! How are you, son?

"Good!"

"That's good. Are the other children close by?"

"Yes, they're here."

"Tell them to come to the phone. I have something to tell all of you."

Blema could hear the clamor in the background as everyone gathered together and huddled around the phone to listen.

"Well, now that you're all together, I want you to know how the much the Lord is blessing us right now. There are a lot of good things happening. How would you feel about coming to the United States?"

"What? What are you talking about, Father?"

"Well, it's much too soon to tell, and I don't want you to get your hopes up too high, but our friends, Ernie Pauline and Jerry Sturgill, have helped us get an attorney to help with immigration. They're all doing everything they can to try to get you here. That is, if you want to come."

There was a short silence before the room exploded with talk and laughter.

"Listen! You need to understand that it's not a sure thing. We have a lot to do in a short amount of time, and it will require us to work together. The attorney, David Purnell, has told us that we will have to submit a DNA sample to US Immigration when we send them our papers. Brother Sturgill has made arrangements for your mother and me to get our tests done here, but we're trying to come up with a way for you to get yours over there. It's going to cost a lot of money—money we don't have right now—so we need you to pray that the Lord will help us and provide a way for us to make this happen. This could be our only chance to ever be together again."

"How much money?" asked Joseph.

"Well, the tests alone will cost about twelve hundred dollars, but then we will have to pay for your travel expenses to get you to Guinea-Conakry and then a place for you to stay once you get there. The tests will have to be done at the US Consulate."

"Oh, my! How will you get that kind of money, Father?"

"I don't know, Joseph. I just know that if the Lord wants you to be here, He will provide the money. We need to pray and trust that it will come, somehow.

CHAPTER 31
Small Miracles

The phone rang several times before Brother Pauline answered it. Brother Sturgill was on the other line.

"Well, Ernie, the Lord works in mysterious ways! There is no doubt in my mind now that He has His hand in this effort."

"Oh, yeah? What's going on, Jerry?"

"Four days ago, we had no idea where we would come up with the money for DNA tests. I'm now sitting here with about two thousand dollars in my hand."

"Really? How is that possible?"

"It just seems that everyone that hears about this story wants to help in some way. The donations have been pouring in. It's unbelievable!"

"That is amazing. Do you want to tell Blema, or do you want me to?"

"I'm afraid that you'll have to. I'm on my way out of town. I wish I could be there, though. I love to see Blema do his little dance whenever he hears good news!"

When Brother Pauline told Blema about the money, Blema was overcome with awe and gratitude. He immediately called his children to share the latest miracle, and to give them travel instructions to Guinea-Conakry.

Overjoyed by the possibility that they might be coming to the United States to be with their parents, the children passed the news on to their uncle, expecting him to share in their excitement. Unfortunately, he did not!

When Mamadou learned of the money, he felt that he was entitled to it. He reasoned that since he had cared for the children in their parents' absence, the money belonged to him. The next day, he called Blema, demanding the money.

"I can't give it to you, Mamadou. I don't have it. Someone else is holding it. Besides that, that money is not mine to give you. It has been donated to help the children immigrate, and it should only be used for that purpose. I don't want to sound ungrateful. Fatoumatou and I feel truly indebted to you and your family for all you have done for the children, but we never wanted to be separated from them. It's only right that they come and be with us now. And besides that, they'll have greater opportunities open to them here."

Mamadou was angry. "You owe me, Blema! If you don't send me the money by the end of the week," he threatened, "the children will no longer be welcome in my home. They will have to find another place to live."

The next time Blema talked with his children, they were staying at the home of a friend, El Hadji Momoudou Bah. Their uncle had forced them out of his home and told them that they could never return.

Devastated, the children called their father. Bangama was crying. Blema was furious when he learned what Mamadou had done. He was worried for the children, but he wasn't sure what to do. Upset and somewhat flustered, Blema called Brother Sturgill and Brother Pauline to tell them of the dilemma.

"I'm sorry, Blema," Brother Sturgill consoled. "That must be hard for the children, but we have to believe that there's a reason for everything. I guess that at this point there's no reason for the children to wait to go on to Conakry. It would be good for them to be close to the embassy anyway. I'm sure that once they get there, the embassy staff can better help them through the process and let them know what they need to do."

Everyone agreed. Brother Sturgill thought that before the children left Labe, it would be a good idea for each of them to obtain an official declaration of birth, assuming that one would be required at the embassy. When he learned that none of them had one, he wasn't quite sure what to do. He opted to draw up an affidavit of birth which would have to be signed by two witnesses of the birth. This could prove to be difficult.

After the affidavits had been prepared, Brother Sturgill called Mr. Bah, whom the children were staying with, and asked him if he might assist them in obtaining the signatures and then take the documents to the court where they would be filed. Mr. Bah agreed, but only if he were paid to do it.

Brother Sturgill sent Mr. Bah the money immediately, and Mr. Bah reported that he had collected the signatures and presented the documents to the court. When Brother Sturgill received a copy of what had been turned in however, he found that important signatures were missing.

When Brother Sturgill questioned Mr. Bah about the documents, he was told that he had done the best he could. He also said that he had never received the money that Brother Sturgill had sent. Brother Sturgill was confused because he had received confirmation that he had. Without the time to get it all straightened out, the decision was made to send the children on to Conakry without the completed affidavits.

One of the greatest concerns the children had about the move to Conakry was finding a place to stay once they got there. The city was filled with violence and corruption, and they were afraid of going there with money in hand to find a place on their own. Brother Sturgill understood their concerns and looked for contacts within the church for help.

Through a series of calls, he was able to connect with Church mission leaders in West Africa who, with permission, gave him the name of a man in Guinea-Conakry. He was one of only thirteen members of the Church in that country. His name was Kpogomon Edouard, a professor at the university and head of the sociology department. Brother Edouard was living with his family in the capital city of Conakry.

"The Church makes the world a small place," Brother Sturgill told Blema. "Isn't it wonderful when we can call upon a brother or sister half way across the world?"

Brother Edouard was surprised to receive the call from the United

States. Brother Sturgill introduced himself and explained the children's situation.

"It sounds like they're going to need some help," Brother Edouard said. "Is there anything I can do?"

"Well, if you have the time, it would be wonderful if you could help them find an apartment or hotel in Conakry, preferably near the embassy."

"I can certainly try, but that might be difficult. There's been a lot of trouble here. We're getting ready to hold an election, and things haven't been going so smoothly. There's been a lot of violence, and prices are extremely high. It could be a challenge to find something that's affordable and safe, but I'll do the best I can."

The next day, the children met Brother Edouard in the city as they had agreed, and for the next few hours, he drove them around the city as they searched for a place to stay. Several places were available, however, the rents were double and sometimes quadruple what they normally were—much more than the children could afford. By the end of the day, they all were worn out and discouraged.

"It seems that we're out of options," Brother Edouard concluded. "I guess that you'll just have to come home with me."

Brother Edouard drove the children to his home where they met his wife and children. The home was nice, built away from the downtown area. The stucco exterior of the house was painted apricot brown and was surrounded by a high wall that was painted the same color. The wall was topped with jagged glass shards, and a guard stood outside. Brother Edouard led the children inside.

The interior of the house was open and spacious but simple and sparsely furnished. Brother Edouard told the children that their house had recently been broken into, and that much of their belongings had been taken. He had been home during the break-in, and in an attempt to protect his things, he had received a stab wound on the top of his head. It had left a scar where his hair now refused to grow. The experience had been frightening for them all and had prompted him to hire an outside guard.

Brother Edouard continued to lead the children through the house. He asked his children to show them to their rooms. Bangama would share a room with Brother Edouard's teenage daughter, while Joseph, Mousa, and Oldpa would share a room in the basement. The children felt comfortable and were glad to be there.

* * * * *

Blema, Brother Sturgill, and Brother Pauline continued to work diligently to move things along on their end; however, they were increasingly concerned about the ticking clock. They now had just over four weeks to meet the deadline.

To help speed things up, Brother Sturgill felt that it would be wise to solicit legal services in Conakry and find someone who knew the immigration process there. Out of ten inquiries that were sent, there was only one response, and that was from a person who lived out of the country and could not help. Although it would be difficult to advise the children from across the globe, Brother Sturgill finally decided that they would just have to do the best they could.

In the meantime, Brother Pauline suggested that each of the children obtain identification cards before going to the embassy in hopes it might facilitate the process once they got there. The others agreed.

Blema called the children to pass the instructions on to them.

"Hello, Joseph?"

"Yes, hello, Father."

"How are you doing? Is everyone all right?"

"Yes, we're fine. We weren't able to find a place to stay, but Brother Edouard has offered to let us stay here with him until we can get things settled."

"Oh, that's wonderful. Brother Edouard is a good man."

"Yes, he is. Did you know that he belongs to the same church as you do?"

"Yes, I heard."

"He's reading the Book of Mormon to us."

"Oh, that makes me happy. Now you'll be prepared to hear the things that I would like to teach you when you get here. You pay attention and listen to all he has to say."

"Yes, Father."

"Tomorrow, you and the others will have to go to the city and try to get an identification card. You'll need it when you go to the embassy. Can you do that?"

"Yes. We'll ask Brother Edouard about transportation, but I'm sure we can."

"Good. If we're going to meet the deadline, you'll have to stay on top of things and do everything that is asked of you. Do you understand?"

"Yes, we will."

"All right. Give the others my love, and tell them I'll talk to them soon."

"We love you too, Father. Good-bye."

CHAPTER 32
Conakry

By mid-morning of their first day in Conakry, the children went to the city to get their identification cards. It had taken all day, but all had received one. The following day, with papers in hand, they went to the embassy where they presented the cards and the less-than-perfect affidavits of birth they had obtained in Labe. The embassy staff took the information and told them they would put it on file. They were also informed that the DNA kits had arrived, and the staff helped them take samples. The samples, they were told, would have to be sent back to the United States for testing.

At the same time, back in Boise, Blema and Fatoumatou had submitted their DNA samples and were waiting for the results.

Before the children left the embassy, each of the children were given a background form to fill out and told they should return them as quickly as possible. The children took the forms but did not understand what was written.

"Do you have these forms in French?" Joseph asked. "We can't read English."

"No, I'm sorry. Those are the only forms we have."

"Is there someone here who can help us translate them?"

"No, I'm afraid not. If you want them translated, you'll have to find someone on your own. You need to know, though, that we can't proceed with your case until the forms have been completed correctly and returned." Another roadblock!

When the children called their father to ask him what they should do, Blema turned to Brother Pauline for help. He was also unsure of what to do and suggested that they pray.

That evening, while searching the Department of Immigration website, Brother Pauline found a copy of the same background form that was given to the children. He thought that if he and Blema could interview the children over the phone, they could fill out the forms for them in English, and then email the completed forms back to them.

Blema thought this was a good idea. The only obstacle was that of finding a good time to make the call. The children would have to receive the call in the morning when they could have access to a phone for a long period of time, but with an eight hour time difference, the call would have to be placed in the middle of the night in Boise. After talking about what they should do, it was agreed that Blema and Fatoumatou would spend the night at the Paulines' house to pull it off.

That evening, Blema and Fatoumatou arrived at the Paulines' house early. While Brother Pauline and Blema were busy in the office preparing the needed forms, Sister Pauline and Fatoumatou were in the kitchen, having a wonderful time preparing dinner for the four of them.

After dinner and a round of pleasant conversation, they all retired early.

At 2:30 in the morning, Brother Pauline and Blema met in the office once again to make the call, and after three hours on the phone, the forms had been completed. The children had then been instructed to find access to a computer where they could print out an emailed copy of the completed forms and take them back to the embassy. The children, however, were afraid to venture into town.

Guinea-Conakry was just three weeks away from holding its first free election since independence.[7] The election would be conducted under a two-round system, with the runoff election scheduled to take place on June 27, 2010.[8] As had been predicted, the election did not run smoothly. Conakry was in turmoil.

Just a year and a half before, a group of protesters had gathered to oppose an attempt by Moussa Camara to become president. When a junta ordered its soldiers to attack, the soldiers had gone on a rampage of rape, mutilation, and murder, and at least fifty-eight people were killed in the clashes.[8]

By the time the children arrived in Conakry, the supporters of twenty-four candidates were gathering in the streets to engender support for their candidate. They were armed with sticks, guns, and machetes. The groups of supporters walked up and down the streets of Conakry, and when one group encountered another, violence often broke out, and there had been several killings.

Each day, the situation seemed to grow worse as Conakry citizens were being caught up in the violence. The children did not feel safe. Brother Edouard advised them and his family to stay in the house unless it was absolutely necessary to venture out for food or supplies. The violence, he hoped, would calm down after the elections.

With only three more weeks to meet the deadline imposed by the immigration office, it was imperative that the forms were returned to the embassy as quickly as possible. The children would not be able to wait until things had settled down. They called their father to ask for his advice.

"Father, we're afraid to go out!" Blema could hear the fear in Joseph's voice.

"I can understand that," Blema told him, "but I'm afraid you have no choice. It's important that you get those papers and take them to the embassy as quickly as you can. I know that it is frightening, but you're going to have to do it. Just go straight there and don't talk to anyone on the way. We'll be praying for you. The Lord will protect you."

The children prayed, as their father had advised, until they had found the courage to venture out. Making their way to the city, they went to where they could get copies made of the completed background forms and then took them to the embassy. Fortunately, they had no trouble. After doing just what was necessary, they went directly back to Brother Edouard's home. Now all they could do was wait.

The outside chaos soon began to affect the lives of everyone in Conakry. Businesses struggled and many were shut down. The university where Brother Edouard taught was also closed down because of the violence, leaving him temporarily without an income. Money became tight.

Having the children in his home and having extra mouths to feed only added to the stresses placed on the family, and tensions ran high. In time, the food that was brought in had to be rationed, and the children often went to bed hungry. It was a difficult time for everyone. Eventually, Brother Edouard felt he could no longer care for the children.

"I'm sorry to have to tell you this," Brother Edouard told them regretfully, "but I'm afraid that you're going to have to find another place to stay. Things have just become too difficult. You can stay here until the end of the month, but after that, I'm afraid you'll have to find another place."

Worried and upset, the children called Blema.

"Father," Mousa asked, "what will happen if we don't meet the deadline and can't get our visas? Where will we go? We're afraid of being stuck here in Conakry with no place to live and no way to take care of ourselves!"

"Listen," Blema told him, "we're not going to worry about that right now. We just need to trust in the Lord. In the meantime, continue to pray and don't lose hope. Tell Brother Edouard I'll be sending him some money to help out. The Lord will keep you safe and provide for you."

CHAPTER 33
Racing a Deadline

Brother Sturgill had become a true champion for the cause of reuniting the Fangamou family, devoting time out of every day to make phone calls and send emails. Although his work had required him to travel during that time, he continued to maintain contact with Mr. Ousman at the US Embassy, the DNA labs staff, Brother Edouard in Conakry, and representatives from the Immigration Agency and World Relief. His tireless efforts kept things moving forward.

The results had come in from the DNA testing, with just two weeks to meet the deadline. There was a problem, however. Although Blema's results showed that it was 99 percent conclusive that he was the father of the children, Fatoumatou's test results were not so clear. The test would have to be done again.

When Brother Pauline delivered the news to Blema and Fatoumatou, Fatoumatou was upset.

"How can that be?" she cried.

"I don't know, Fatoumatou. I guess there could be many possible reasons the results weren't clear. I know you've had several blood transfusions and have been taking medication for blood-borne illnesses. Who knows? We'll just have to do it again."

"Is there time?" asked Blema.

"I don't know. That could be a problem."

Fatoumatou began to cry.

"This isn't looking good!" said Blema. "If things don't work out and we can't get the visas, Fatoumatou and I will have to find a way to go back to Africa. Our children need us there. We don't want to be separated from them any longer."

Brother Pauline looked at Blema and then to Fatoumatou and felt sorry for them. He wanted to say something to comfort them, but he didn't know what. He put his arm around Fatoumatou's shoulders. Suddenly, a strong impression came to his mind and he felt compelled to declare, "Fatoumatou, in the name of the living God, you will soon hold your children in your arms."

Fatoumatou buried her face into his shoulder and sobbed.

* * * * *

Brother Pauline spoke to Brother Sturgill and Brother Purnell about the test results. Since there was not enough time to retake the tests, they decided to send only the paternity test results with the written response that would be submitted by June 29th. Brother Sturgill would instruct them concerning the maternity test results on a later date.

With the groundwork laid and all the vital information gathered, Brother Sturgill and Brother Purnell began drafting the written response. Kathy Bettger, a retired French teacher who had volunteered with the IRC, had been helpful in obtaining many of the details about Blema and Fatoumatou's experience in Guinea-Bissau that would be used in the written response.

By June 23rd, Brother Sturgill and Brother Purnell had come up with a final draft. There were only six days left to meet the deadline. Brother Purnell requested that Blema come into his office the next day to review it.

On Thursday, June 24th, Blema met him in his office at 8:30 a.m. The two of them spent all morning and much of the afternoon going over the details of the response. By late afternoon, Brother Sturgill and Brother Pauline had joined them.

After all they had done to prepare the draft, they felt that something was still not quite right. All agreed that the document was not as compelling as they would like it to be. At the last minute, they decided to take a completely different approach and rewrite the draft.

On Friday, June 25th, with four days left, the men worked on the revision of the final draft until it was complete. Brother Pauline called the Immigration Department to confirm the address to where the response should be sent.

With the response written, the packets were now ready to be put together. A separate packet would have to be prepared for each child, which would include copies of all the documents and evidences to support the case. These would require some time to be put together.

Since the package would have to go out no later than Monday to arrive by overnight delivery on Tuesday the 29th, Brother Pauline suggested that they meet together the next day, on Saturday, to finish preparing the packets. All agreed.

On Saturday, June 26th, Brother Pauline, Brother Sturgill, Brother Purnell, along with his wife, Elizabeth, and his son Michael, all met together to help prepare the packets. Over the next few hours, hundreds of copies were made of the required information. Brother Purnell and Brother Sturgill finalized the editing of the draft.

With all of the copies made, the half-inch thick packets were put together in a package. The package was then sealed and addressed. By late afternoon, the package was complete and ready to be sent out. Everyone gathered one last time to pray.

Brother Purnell offered the prayer. Brother Pauline reached out and put his hand on the package as Brother Purnell proceeded to pray.

In his prayer, he asked the Lord for three specific things. First, he asked that the packets would arrive safely on Monday, June 28th, the day before the deadline. Second, he asked that the packet would be placed in the hands of a compassionate person who would feel an urgency to work with the case. His final request was that the applications would be approved and the children would receive their visas as quickly as possible. The prayer was closed with five heartfelt "Amens." That evening, the packages were sent.

The following Monday, Brother Pauline called Terri MacDonald with the Agency for New Americans to tell her that the package had been sent, and to ask her how long they should expect to wait for the response.

"Well, typically it takes about three months," she replied, "but it could take as long as six, or even longer."

Seventeen days later, on July 15th, Brother Purnell was informed that the department had received the packets a day early. After careful review, the children had been approved to receive their visas.

* * * * *

"Hello, Joseph?" Blema said, trying to keep his voice from giving away his excitement. "Get the others. Your mother and I have some news."

When everyone had gathered around the phone, Blema began, "Well. . ."

Before Blema could say another word, Fatoumatou snatched the phone from him. "You've been approved!" she cried through the mouthpiece. "You'll be coming home to us!"

Shouts of excitement could be heard over the phone, and many tears were shed. After twelve years of separation, it seemed that they would be together once again.

CHAPTER 34
Bringing Them Home

Wherefore . . . there shall none come into this land
save they shall be brought by the hand of the Lord.
2 Nephi 1:6

It was now the first week of August. The children had been approved to receive their visas, but they soon found out that the approval was only the first hurdle. The lengthy process of actually obtaining them was still ahead.

Although the process would typically take about two months, no one was quite certain how long it would be. Brother Edouard had allowed the children to live at his home until he knew that they had been approved for their visas, but regrettably, his personal circumstances would not allow them to stay with him any longer.

Brother Sturgill called Brother Edouard to thank him and his family for caring for the children.

"Is there anything I can do for you?" Brother Sturgill asked.

"Yes, there is one thing," he replied. "Would you place our names on the prayer roll at the temple? We will need those prayers."

"Yes, of course I will."

Brother Sturgill was touched by Brother Edouard's humble response. Thinking of all that this good man had been through over the past few months, and of all of the sacrifices that had been made to bring the children into his home, when Brother Sturgill had hung up the phone, he sat in his chair and wept.

With concern for the children, Brother Sturgill began making inquiries to Church leaders in West Africa, hoping to find another situation where they could be watched over by Church members. After several phone calls, he learned that the closest members were in Ghana. This would be a safer place for the children, but it was not practical. It was important for them to remain in Conakry near the embassy until their immigration status was firm. The children would have no choice but to stay there.

With donations that he had helped gather, Brother Sturgill sent money to the children to allow them to rent an apartment in the city. After a long day of searching, the children found an apartment that they thought they could afford in the downtown area. Unfortunately, the area had become unsafe.

The political turmoil in Conakry that had plagued the country for months continued. With runoff elections over, the country was now preparing for the second round election, which was scheduled for July 18, 2010.[9]

The election that was to take place on July 18th did not happen due to allegations of electoral fraud and a need to calm the violence. The election was rescheduled for September 19th.

The candidates had been narrowed down to two: Cellou Diallo, who represented mostly members of the Puel (Fula) tribe, and Alpha Conde, who represented many of the Malinke (Mandinka) tribe. Over the years, the animosity that once existed between the Fula and Mandinka tribes had returned, and this contest only underscored the divisions between the tribes and further set them against one another. The incidents of violence within the city had increased, and most of them had occurred in the downtown area.

Afraid to venture out, the children holed themselves up in their apartment.

"Father, we can't stay here!" Bangama sobbed during one of the daily phone calls to her parents. "Why is it taking so long? Why can't we just come now? We're afraid!"

"We're doing all we can, Bangama," her father consoled. "Things always take longer than we think they should. Are you staying close to the apartment?"

"Yes. We only go out when we have to, but there's nothing for us to do here. We've been hearing gunfire near our apartment at night. We've all been sleeping under our mattresses so we won't get hit. We just want to come now! How much longer will it be?"

"I don't know, Bangama. You'll have to be strong. Everyone is doing all they can, but no one can say how long it will be. The Lord is watching over you. Do you believe that?"

"Yes, Father."

"Good! I'll call you again tomorrow."

One week before the September election, the president of the National Independent Electoral Commission was convicted of vote tampering during the first round of voting. The election was again postponed until November 7th.[10] The threat of violence remained.

Weeks went by without hearing anything from the embassy. In late September, the children were called in because of questions that were being raised about the background forms that they had provided weeks before.

When they arrived at the embassy, a man named Cici met them at the door and told them that certain forms they had turned in previously had been filled out wrong. He offered to redo the forms and fill them out correctly, but it would cost them one hundred and fifty dollars. Trusting that he was telling them the truth, Joseph paid him seventy-five dollars, part of the money they had been sent for food and rent.

The next day, Brother Sturgill called Ousman at the embassy and asked about the incident. Ousman told him that there had not been a problem with the forms. The children had been robbed. They were advised to hold on to their money.

Brother Sturgill worked closely with Ousman, hoping to hurry the case along, but progress was slow. It seemed that for every step forward, there were two steps back.

Ousman had informed him that they were still waiting for the files from the US State Department, and that they could not move forward until they had received them. It took several weeks to discover that when the US State Department had sent a required notice of action to Blema to be signed and returned, they had sent it to an old address, and Blema did not receive it. It then took several more weeks to correct the problem.

In October, the embassy requested the chain of custody documentation from the DNA testing lab as it related to Blema's paternity test. Copies were sent via email, but the embassy required the physical documents. The embassy could not issue the visas until the documentation was received. The forms were prepared and sent out immediately.

By November, it seemed that things were finally moving along when Ousman informed Brother Sturgill that he was taking an assignment away from the embassy and would be gone for about a month. This would delay things once again!

On November 7th, the final election took place in Conakry as scheduled. Many had hoped that this would bring an end to the violence, but it did not.

When Alpha Conde was declared to be the winner of the election, Puel supporters began to riot. Shortly after the election, they were in the streets burning tires, barricading the roads, and destroying the homes and businesses of their Malinke neighbors. Groups of men lined the road from the capital to the suburbs, shaking sticks, guns, and machetes at the passing cars. During the riots, four people were killed and sixty-two were injured.[11]

On November 18th, the Guinean military declared a state of emergency. Only the military would be allowed unrestricted movement. The citizens could go to work or to the market, but they were required to travel alone and not move in groups. A curfew was set for 7:00 p.m.

"Father!" Bangama cried over the phone. "How much longer? Things are really crazy here; we can't go anywhere. We just want to get out of here!"

"I know things are frightening, but things are starting to come together at the embassy," Blema reassured. "You'll come soon."

"You've said that before, Father, many times, but nothing's happening! Maybe they've been lying to you. I'm afraid we're going to die here!"

"Calm down, Bangama! You're going to be all right. Just be patient a little while longer. The Lord is protecting you. You'll come soon. There are many people here praying for you, people you don't even know. You'll have to be patient."

Two weeks later, on December 3rd, the children were at a point of despair when they were requested to come to the embassy once again.

"Well, we have some good news for you!" announced an embassy staff woman as they walked through the Embassy doors. "Your visas are here!"

The children could hardly believe what they were hearing. Bangama let out a squeal of excitement.

"We've contacted World Relief and they have given us assurance that they are now ready to receive you." the woman continued. "You'll have to go through a medical screening and receive the required inoculations, but then you'll be cleared to go. Unless there are any unforeseen problems, you'll fly out on December 13th. "

When Blema and Fatoumatou heard from their children that the visas had been issued and travel arrangements had been made, they were ecstatic.

"We have a lot to be thankful for," Blema told them over the phone. "Soon you'll be getting on the plane and coming here. We'll be together again! Your mother and I are so happy and thankful; we don't have the words to express it. When we were in the camp, we thought we might not ever see you again. The Lord has answered our prayers. We've seen a lot of miracles, but this . . . this is the greatest one of all."

They all agreed.

"I'll be sending you money for shoes and haircuts," he went on. "You can all share a travel bag . . . and try to find warm coats. It's very cold here."

Blema was concerned about the children's safety while going out to get those things, but they reassured him that the violence had calmed down over the past couple of weeks, and they were sure they would be fine.

December 13th, the day of the children's departure, finally arrived. The children were filled with anxious anticipation as they made their final preparations to leave. Arrangements had been made for them to be picked up from their apartment at nine o'clock that night and taken to the airport. Their plane was scheduled to leave at eleven o'clock. They would make stops in Paris and Chicago and then arrive in Boise at 10:16 p.m. the following day.

* * * * *

"Can you remember what Mother looks like?" Bangama asked Mousa as they were putting their things together.

"Not really; it's been too long. I just remember that she's very tall."

"I just can't believe that we are finally going to see them again. I don't know if I am more excited or scared!"

Bangama went into the bathroom and was there for a long time. Before long, her brothers were pounding on the door, wanting to get in.

"Bangama, get out of there!" they exclaimed impatiently. "What's taking you so long?"

When Bangama finally came out of the bathroom, she explained, "Someone told me once that I look like my father. I've been looking at my face in the mirror so when I see him, I'll recognize him."

* * * * *

Blema and Fatoumatou were filled with emotion and had been counting the hours until they would see their children again. Three hours before the children's flight was due to arrive, however, Brother Pauline received a disturbing call from World Relief.

"I'm afraid that we can't locate the children," they said. "Their flight was scheduled to arrive at the Chicago airport at 6:51, but the flight never arrived. No one seems to know where they are."

When Brother Pauline told Blema what had happened, he felt sick. Brother Pauline called Brother Sturgill to tell him what had happened.

"What do you mean they've lost them?" Brother Sturgill exclaimed. "How can that be?"

"I don't know; it's crazy!" exclaimed Brother Pauline.

"I don't know where to start looking," said Brother Sturgill. "Would you mind calling everyone that was planning on coming to the airport tonight and tell them the children won't be coming. I'm going to make some phone calls and try to get some answers."

Brother Sturgill began by making a call to Travelers Aid at the O'Hare airport in Chicago. After looking into it, they informed him that children's flight had been cancelled due to snowstorms. They had no more information.

Thinking that perhaps the plane never left Guinea-Conakry, he made a call to the airport there, but there was no answer. He continued making calls to various locations throughout the evening, but each call had led him to a dead end. By 11:00 p.m., he felt that he had exhausted all of the possibilities. He called Blema to report.

"I'm really sorry, Blema. No one seems to know anything. I'm afraid I've done all that I can do."

Brother Sturgill could feel the deafening silence on the other end of the line.

"You know, I do have one more thought," Brother Sturgill said after desperately trying to come up with something to provide some hope. "I have the number to the IOM headquarters in Geneva, Switzerland. Perhaps I'll give them a try. I'll have to wait until morning to make the call, so until then, let's try to get some sleep."

"Thank you," Blema managed. "Thank you for all you've done."

Sleep did not come easy that night for Blema and Fatoumatou. They were beside themselves with worry.

By 4:30 the next morning, Brother Sturgill was on the phone to the IOM office in Switzerland. Chantelle answered the phone. Brother Sturgill was pleased learn that she had the information he had been looking for.

"The children's connecting flight in Chicago was cancelled due to the snowstorm," Chantelle explained. "The flight was redirected to New York. The children have been put up in a hotel there, and their flight to Boise has been rescheduled for the sixteenth. I have the number to the hotel, would you like to take it down?"

"Of course!" Brother Sturgill exclaimed. "Thank you very much. This is going to make a couple of people very happy."

Just as soon as he hung up the phone, Brother Sturgill called Blema to tell him the good news. The children had not been lost after all, just delayed. Blema and Fatoumatou were anxious to speak with them.

With Blema still on the line, Brother Sturgill initiated a three-way call to the hotel. A woman with a pleasant voice answered the phone as she sat at the front desk, and Brother Sturgill asked her to connect him with the children's room.

As the phone rang, Brother Sturgill and Blema listened, but there was no answer. After waiting a few minutes, they tried again, but there was still no answer. After several calls, Brother Sturgill called the front desk again and asked the woman if she would mind going up to the room and check on the children.

"Of course, I would be happy to," she replied.

When she arrived and knocked on the door, Mousa timidly came to the door and opened it. The woman greeted him and asked him if they had heard the phone ring. Mousa nodded in the affirmative, but the woman suspected that he had not understood her English. She walked into the room and picked up the phone to show the boys how to use it. They watched closely, and then nodded enthusiastically to reassure her that they had understood.

It was not long before the phone rang once again, and this time, Joseph picked it up.

"Hello, Joseph?" said Blema.

"Yes, hello Father!"

"Brother Sturgill is on the phone with me. We were worried about you. Is everyone all right?"

"Yes, we're fine. We're here in a big hotel in New York."

"Yes, I know. I'm sorry about the delay. How is everyone?"

"I guess they're all right. Mousa is here with me, but I haven't seen Bangama and Oldpa since we got here. They were put in a different room."

"I have their room number," said Brother Sturgill. "They should be in the room next to yours. Would you like to go check on them?"

"No . . . I can't."

"Why not?"

"I'll get lost. Then no one will ever find me!"

Blema and Brother Sturgill reassured Joseph and the others that everything would be all right, and that they would be safely in Boise on Thursday.

On Thursday, December 16th, IOM representatives in New York arranged for the children to be at the LaGuardia Airport in time to board the plane for their 5:05 p.m. flight. After their connecting flights, they would fly on to Boise. Arrival time: 10:46 p.m.

* * * * *

In Boise, Blema and Fatoumatou began counting the hours once again. Many other people were anticipating the children's arrival as well. Blema and Fatoumatou had many friends and supporters who had grown to love them, and they rejoiced with them that the long separation with their children was about to come to an end.

That night, when Brother and Sister Pauline arrived at Blema and Fatoumatou's apartment to pick them up and take them to the airport, they were ready and waiting. Blema was standing at the door, dressed in a white shirt and tie. Fatoumatou stood next to him, wearing a dress and a beautiful wig that she wore only on special occasions.

"Well," asked Sister Pauline, "are you ready for this?"

"Oh, yes!" Blema exclaimed.

"*Oui*!" said Fatoumatou, smiling broadly.

"This is a good day!" Blema added. "A very good day!"

"Well, if everyone is ready," said Brother Pauline, "what are we waiting for? Let's go!"

Arriving at the airport early, Brother Pauline and Blema checked the flights to make sure they were still scheduled to arrive on time. Brother Pauline was carrying a brown paper bag filled with small American flags and colorful leis to present to the children when they arrived. Blema carried flowers that he had bought for Bangama. Everyone made their way to the arrival gate to wait.

Before long, others started to show up. Brother and Sister Sturgill walked in and greeted Blema and Fatoumatou.

"Well," Brother Sturgill said. "This is it! The day we've been waiting for!"

Bishop and Sister Stevens soon joined them, along with other friends. Brother and Sister Purnell were there with their son Michael. Nate Lacey came with his wife and other World Relief staff.

Over the next half hour, they were also joined by Christine Briscoe, Larry and Katie Lim, Ralph and Lorraine Ball, Bob and Brenda Young, and Greg and Vicky Rasmussen. The Pauline's son, Ryan, was there to take pictures.

As the time of arrival drew closer, Blema and Fatoumatou stood in front of the doors and watched. Their eyes did not leave the doors.

For the next twenty minutes, every time a flight would come in, everyone looked to see if the children were among the passengers. After several flights, they began to wonder if perhaps the children had been lost again.

Finally, flight 6395 landed. Blema and Fatoumatou watched closely as the passengers made their way through the gate. Suddenly, the door opened and Oldpa appeared. Jolted by the excitement of seeing their son, Blema and Fatoumatou ran toward him. Fatoumatou reached him first. She grabbed him and hugged him so tightly that they both nearly toppled over.

Blema came to greet Oldpa as Mousa came through the gate. Fatoumatou went to Mousa and embraced him, laughing and smiling, as tears streamed down her face.

Bangama was next. When Fatoumatou and Bangama saw one another, they fell into each other's arms and wept. Joseph joined them and held them both.

Blema greeted each child as they came in. He was also crying. He embraced each of his boys, firmly patting them on the back. When Bangama came to him, he held her for a moment and then, while still holding her hands, stepped back to look at her. Pulling her back against him, he held her tightly. He then presented her with the flowers he had brought.

Everyone who had come to greet the children welcomed them with leis and flags as they came through. When the family finally gathered together for a picture, the crowd broke out into applause.

Brother Pauline came to Blema to congratulate him. In the excitement of the moment he exclaimed, "We serve a powerful God!"

"The Lord Jesus Christ!" Blema replied.

Brother Pauline then went to Fatoumatou, and while holding both of her hands he looked into her eyes and said, "Fatoumatou, do you remember the promise you were given months ago . . . that you would soon hold your children in your arms once again?"

"*Oui*," she answered tearfully.

"Well, I believe today that promise has been fulfilled!"

Fatoumatou looked over at each of her children and smiled. "My children are here," she exclaimed in French. "We'll never be separated again!"

* * * * *

God doesn't write with a pen . . . "not with ink, but with the Spirit of the living God; not in tables of stone, but in fleshy tables of the heart."

—2 Corinthians 3:3

Epilogue

With the help of World Relief, Joseph, Mousa, and Oldpa were set up in an apartment a few doors down from where their parents live. Bangama moved in with her mother and father where she occupies the loft bedroom.

One of the first things the children did after arriving in America was to change their names to the Christian equivalent of their African names. Bangama now goes by Elise, Joseph is still Joseph, and Mousa changed his name to Moses. Oldpa now goes by Emmanuel.

All of the children began taking English classes immediately after their arrival to the United States. Each has caught on quickly to the new language.

Elise and Moses are both attending Borah High School, where Elise is a sophomore and Moses is a junior. Elise enjoys school and has won the hearts of her teachers and the school principal. She has maintained good grades and has been awarded a certificate for excellence in literacy. Elise also enjoys cooking and sewing, and she loves to spend time with the young women at church.

Moses is also doing well in school. He especially likes being part of the school choir. He enjoys playing soccer and hopes to be part of the school team next year. Moses is employed at the Riverside Inn in Boise where he washes dishes at night and on Saturdays.

Joseph is employed by Deseret Industries where he is learning job and English language skills. Deseret Industries has also provided him an opportunity to take a driver's training course and has assisted him in acquiring a driver's license.

Joseph has also worked with Kenny Kartchner in his window washing business, and for Western Building Maintenance, cleaning offices at night.

Emmanuel took a job at a dairy in Oregon for several months, where he worked long hours and often sent money to his parents to help them out. He has now returned to Boise where he is employed with Five Guys Burgers and Fries on 8th Street as well as Riverside Inn. He enjoys playing soccer with his brothers and friends.

Blema and Fatoumatou enjoy their role as parents to their young adult children.

Excited to have their children learn the gospel, Blema and Fatoumatou began teaching them immediately after they arrived. The children were receptive to their parents' teachings as Blema and Fatoumatou shared with them the truths that they had come to cherish. Arrangements were made for the missionaries to teach the children as well.

On February 17, 2011, all four children were baptized and confirmed as members of the Church of Jesus Christ of Latter-day Saints. Since then, Joseph, Moses, and Emmanuel have received the Aaronic Priesthood, and Elise and her brothers were able to go the temple and participate in the sacred ordinance of baptism for the dead.

Blema received the Melchizedek Priesthood on November 7, 2010, and on September 21, 2011, he was able to take Fatoumatou to the Twin Falls Temple where their marriage was sealed for time and all eternity. They are looking forward to doing genealogy work and to performing saving ordinances in the temple in behalf of their ancestors.

Blema is still working at Wal-Mart, in the produce department.

As Blema was leaving the Kpomasse camp, a man had come up to him and said, "You know, this reminds me of the story of Joseph of old. Just before the butler left the prison, Joseph told him, 'Think on me when it shall be well with thee.' So it is with you, Blema . . . remember us." To this, Blema answered, "I will."

Blema did not forget. His friend's words continued to work on Blema's heart after he had arrived in the United States. He felt inspired to start a clinic in Labe, Africa. The Feel Better Clinic was opened April

20, 2012. It employs five doctors, two nurses, a pharmacist, and an accountant. He is now working with the Labe government to open a second clinic in that region. Blema feels that this service is fulfilling the promise he made with his people.

Blema and Fatoumatou's oldest sons, Kamonan and Sekouna, were too old to immigrate with the other children under their parents' refugee status, and they remain in Africa. Sekouna helps maintain the clinic in Labe, while Kamonan is a painter in Conakry. Blema and Fatoumatou hope that they will see them again someday.

Blema and Fatoumatou would like to give thanks to all who have given their help and support since their arrival in the United States. Most important, they would like to give praise and glory to their Father in Heaven, who has kept His promises to them, and for the miracle of life.

In Blema's Own Words

A TESTIMONY

My testimony is very simple. Since I became a Christian, and since I had to flee from my country to come to another country, I have come to believe in a God of miracles. Today, many are in doubt that they have a God of miracles. I have no doubt.

The first time I realized a miracle in my life was when I didn't die in the pharmacy. I will always share this with every believer and nonbeliever. This experience shows that we have a God of miracles.

What did I do to have miracles? I had to repent. I had to have faith in the Lord; no doubt. I have no doubt because Jesus is able. I don't fear because my life is in the hand of the Lord. I never lose hope. I always bring happiness into my life, even in the times of difficulty and in times of trials, because I know that Jesus is with me, and He is able. In the morning, I thank the Lord, always. I cry with those that cry.

While we were in the camp, one of the refugees, a young man from Chad, was surrounded by many Ogoni refugees. They attacked him. They beat him and kicked him and cut him with a machete. He was taken to the hospital, but the doctors told him, "We have no sympathy for fighting. You bring money, or have your parents bring money, and then we will take care of you, otherwise, if you die, you die." The parents had nothing.

Fatoumatou and I had been saving a little money and would use it to buy food. When I saw the young man, I asked Fatoumatou if we could help the man, and she agreed. I said, "We will live with hunger, but even if we have nothing, we have to share equally." I went to the hospital and gave the doctors our money. I told them if it wasn't enough, I would pay the rest. That is what I believe the Book of Mormon teaches us.

In the Book of Mormon, Mosiah 18:9 tells us that we are to cry with those that cry, and I know that the Book of Mormon is a book of truth.

My conclusion is that the Lord is good! The Lord protects me. The Lord guides me and He saves me. He brought me out of trial and has given me peace. The Lord was very kind to me and showed me this church. It has changed me and blessed me. I have this miracle.

The greatest miracle I have in my life? The man who died in Calvary. He has done it for me; in my life, in your life, in everybody's life.

I would exhort everyone to believe in the Lord and to believe that the Lord is good, and that the Book of Mormon is true, and that Joseph Smith is a prophet. No one told me this is true. I prayed about it, and this knowledge was revealed to me. It is true. I tell you these things in the name of Jesus Christ, Amen.

PHOTOS

Blema and Fatoumatou

Fangamou family picture: left to right,
Emanuel, Elise, Blema, Fatoumatou, Moses, and Joseph.

Blema and Fatoumatou at the Idaho Falls Temple
on the day of their sealing.

Blema and Fatoumatou with Brother and Sister Pauline at the Idaho Falls Temple.

Fangamou family at the children's baptisms. From left to right: Joseph, Moses, Emanuel, Elise, Fatoumatou, and Blema.

Joseph working at Deseret Industries.

Joseph at Deseret Industries with Kristen Richards, development specialist, and Brent Perkins, job specialist.

Moses playing soccer.

Emanuel in his Five Guys work shirt.

Elise

The four amigos: Jerry Sturgill, Blema Fangamou, David Purnell, and Ernie Pauline.

Blema and Brother Pauline.

Feel Better Clinic in Labe.

The Feel Better Clinic provides medical services to families that could not afford it otherwise. Over 10 percent of the patients seen last year were given free medical care.

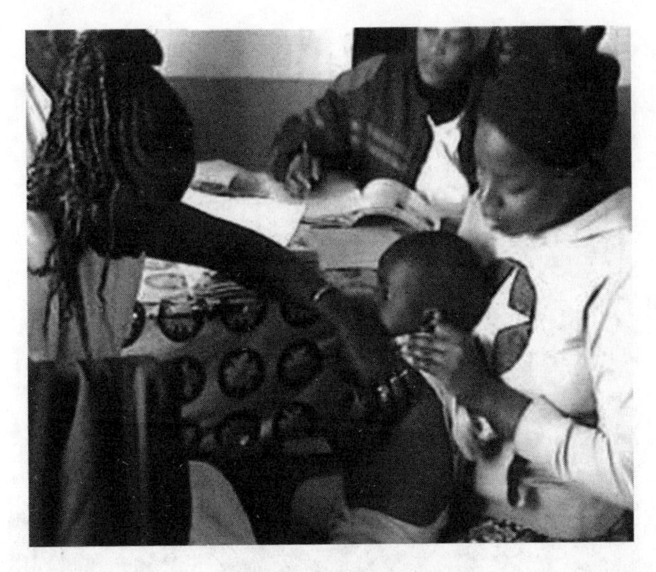

Infants and children are vaccinated against threatening disease, including malaria and intestinal parasites.

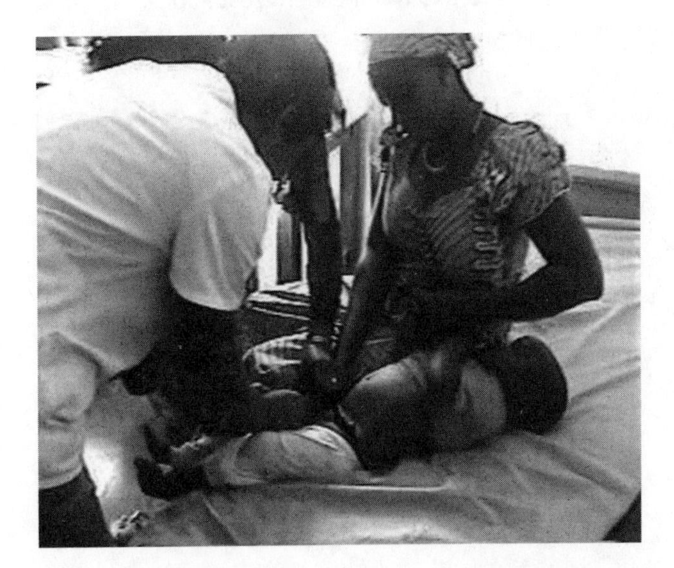

In the first eight months of operation, the Feel Better Clinic served 2,343 patients, including 116 live births.

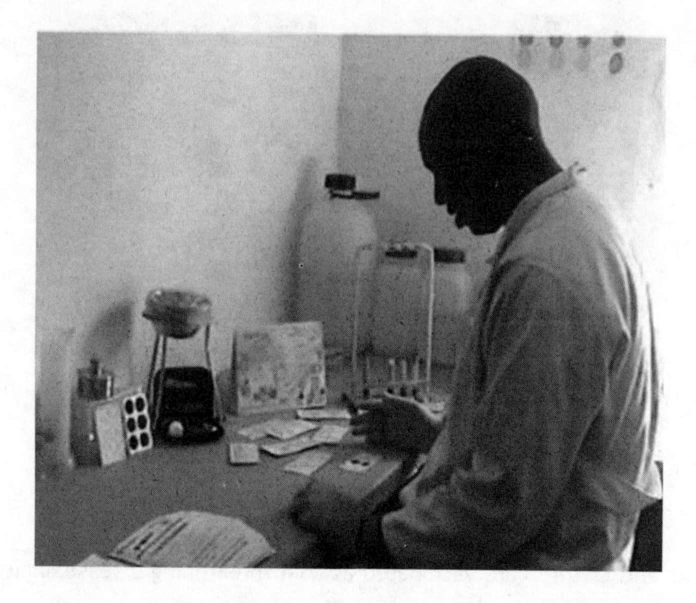

Some of the regions most capable doctors are employed at the Feel Better Clinic in Labe, West Africa.

NOTES

Chapter 2

1 "History of the Mandingo Tribe," Gaynor Borade, last modified February 17, 2012, www.buzzle.com.

2 "Mandinka People," livingpearl, last modified February 17, 2012, www.blackethics.com.

Chapter 4

3 "Guinea-Bissau Rights and Liberties Report," last modified 2010, www.old.freedomhouse.org/template.cfm?page=228country=8049&year=2011.

4 PAIGC, *Jornal No Pintcha*, 29 November 1980: In a statement in the part newspaper No Pintcha (In the Vanguard), a spokesman for the PAIGC revealed that many of the ex-Portuguese indigenous African soldiers that were executed after cessation of hostilities were buried in unmarked collective graves in the woods of Cumera, Portogole, and Mansala.

5 "Guinea-Bissau Introduction-2006," *The World Factbook 2006* (Washington D.C., 2006), www.cia.gov/library/publications/the-world-factbook/index.html.

Chapter 9

6 "RESPECT Volunteer visits Benin Refugee Camp," *RESPECT e-Zine*, September 22, 2006, www.theodora.com/wfbcurrent/guineabissau/guineabissau_introduction.html.

Chapter 32

7 "Guinea Holds 1st Free Election; Military Rule Dissolves with Democratic Vote," Todd Pitman, June 28, 2010, www.ap.org.

8 "At Least 58 Killed in Guinea Opposition Protest," Courtest; Voice of America, September 29, 2009, accessed through Mandingo Nations Website.

Chapter 34

9 "Guinea-Conakry, Presidential Election Run-Off (Second Round)," Consultancy Africa Intelligence, Hanna Gibson, October 2010.

10 "Situation of Human Rights Defenders," FIDH, last modified January 27, 2012, accessed June 28, 2012, www.fidh.org/GUINEA-CONAKRY-2010-2011.

11 "Guinea Declares State of Emergency Amid Post-Election Violence," Nicholas Germain, last modified November 17, 2010, www.france24.com/en/20101117-guinea-declares-state-emergency-amid-election-violence-alpha-conde-sekouba-konate%20.

ACKNOWLEDGMENTS

When the idea of writing this book was conceived, I could never have imagined how many people would eventually become involved to make it a reality. I feel extremely blessed to have been surrounded by the wonderfully supportive and talented people who have so kindly overlooked my inadequacies and inexperience and helped me along the way. I would like express my gratitude and give credit where credit is due.

First of all, my thanks go to Blema and Fatoumatou Fangamou. It is a rare thing when you find people of such pure faith that they make you feel closer to God whenever you are near them. I appreciate your sweet friendship and your willingness to open your lives to me. I have learned much from your simple, yet powerful, acts of faith.

I could not have written this book without the support of my family. They have buoyed me up at times when I felt that I could not finish and have shown great patience and understanding, even during times of serious neglect. Thank you for your confidence in me. I love and appreciate you more than you will ever know.

To my good husband, Ernie, who patiently endured many a lonely hour while encouraging me to write; I appreciate the way you have stood by my side and believed in me. Your unfailing support has meant the world to me. You are my steady rock and the love of my life. I adore you.

Jonah Pauline, the cover photo you have created has been described to me as "stunning," and truly it is. The map design is equally as impressive. You have an amazing talent and a giving heart, and you have been generous in sharing both. Thank you.

To Ray Beers, Christine Briscoe, Sandy Claiborne, Angie Ebeltoft, Sharon Garland, Kathy Kartchner, Brunell Lee, Katie Lim, Louise Miller, Beci Ramage, and Rachael Reed and Jo Rhodus, who were not only willing, but enthused to be my first readers; thank you so much. Your suggestions have been invaluable. To Ann Skinner and Carol Shults, thank you for sharing your editing skills and for helping to prepare the manuscript for submission. I could not have done this without you.

Thank you, Laurel Day, for providing "The Four Amigos" photo; Lindsay Hendriks of Steele Photography, for the author photo; Lisa Schulz for permission to use your beautiful picture of Fatoumatou, taken at the World Refugee Day celebration; and Steve Mendenhall, for providing graphic design for printed materials and creative video for book trailers. All of you are amazingly gifted and wonderful people.

Many, many thanks to the talented staff at Cedar Fort, Inc. It has been a pleasure and delight to work with all of you. I would like to give special acknowledgment and thanks to Steve Acevedo, marketing publicist, for all of his enthusiasm, encouragement, and never-ending support. He has become a dear friend who has shared our vision for this project and has worked tirelessly to help us achieve success. Thank you, Angie Workman, acquisitions editor, for leading me through the initial process of publication, Rebecca Greenwood for your help with website design and preliminary cover design, Shawnda Craig, for the final cover design, and Emily Chambers, my wonderful editor, for your patience and uplifting comments, and to all others who have contributed to this book.

I would also like to thank John H. Groberg, Greg Olsen, John Lund, and Sara Wells for your kind and complimentary endorsements. I have great respect and admiration for each of you, and I feel honored that you have taken the time to read and endorse this work.

Most important, I would like to thank my Heavenly Father, for it is through Him that all things are possible.

About the Author

CHRISTI LYNN PAULINE was born in the humble town of Blackfoot, Idaho, near the Fort Hall Indian reservation. It was here that her interest in other cultures was cultivated at an early age. Her love of God, people, and literature has fueled a desire to write, and her favorite subject is that of ordinary people who possess extraordinary faith. She enjoys reading and writing poetry and has authored a children's book entitled, *Hullaballoo at the Zoo*.

Christi currently resides in Meridian, Idaho, with her husband, Ernie, where they are both serving as ward missionaries for The Church of Jesus Christ of Latter-day Saints. They also serve as ordinance workers in the Boise Idaho Temple. As a wife, mother, and grandmother, Christi treasures time spent with her family.

0 26575 11732 5